Mothering in Hip-Hop Culture

Representation and Experience

Mothering in Hip-Hop Culture

Representation and Experience

Edited by

Maki Motapanyane

DEMETER

DEMETER PRESS

Published by:
Demeter Press
c/o Motherhood Initiative for Research and
 Community Involvement (MIRCI)
140 Holland St. West, P.O. 13022
Bradford, ON, L3Z 2Y5
Telephone: 905.775.9089
Email: info@demeterpress.org
Website: www.demeterpress.org

Demeter Press logo based on Skulptur "Demeter" by Maria-Luise Bodirsky
<www.keramik-atelier.bodirsky.edu>

Printed and Bound in Canada

Library and Archives Canada Cataloguing in Publication

        Mothering in hip-hop culture : representation and experience /
edited by Maki Motapanyane.

Includes bibliographical references.
ISBN 978-1-927335-00-0

Cataloguing data available from Library and Archives Canada.

For Maia and Terence

Table of Contents

Acknowledgements

I EXTEND MY DEEPEST GRATITUDE to the women who have been an inspiration for this book: Roxanne Shanté, Lady P, Michie Mee, Motion, Martha Diaz, Helixx C. Armageddon, Pri the Honeydark, Mel Boogie, M.I.A., Rachel Raimist and countless others who, in subtle and sometimes more obvious ways, reflect the enriching and productive force of motherhood in Hip-Hop culture.

A special word of thanks is also due to the contributors of this volume for their insightful scholarship and appreciation for the relevance of studious rumination on the dynamics of motherhood in Hip-Hop. Thank you to contributors Shana Calixte and Mark Campbell for securing those rare interviews with our Canadian artists, and to Shana for your unfaltering interest and support in this project from the very beginning.

I also extend my thanks to the press editors, and particularly Andrea O'Reilly and Renée Knapp, for their support and foresight when this volume was just an idea. There were some hiccups along the way in sustaining the research institute, but the tenacity with which you have insisted on securing a space for research on motherhood as well as nurturing a community of scholars is admirable to say the least.

A particular word of thanks goes out to the friends, colleagues, and mentors who have sustained me these past few years: Emily Rosser, Shihoko Nakagawa, Jennifer Johnson, Rai Reece, Dana Guyton, Penny Weiss and Bettina Bradbury. In addition, my love and deepest appreciation to my family—my children Maia and Terence, and my parents, Virginia and Rod.

Introduction

Motherhood Between Invisibility and Trope

MAKI MOTAPANYANE

THIS COLLECTION EMERGES from a personal fascination with the tenuous position of motherhood in the expressive forms of Hip-Hop culture. In a practical sense, motherhood is ever present—artists negotiate relationships of mutuality or alienation with their mothers, some of the women among them become mothers themselves in the midst of a busy professional career, and those who are fathers are linked to the mothers of their children through the attendant social and moral expectations if not through partnership and direct interaction. In addition and more generally speaking, Hip-Hop remains a site of identification and connection, and of contention and distance between Black parents and their children. Mothers share the music with children and/or worry about the appropriateness and influence of content on children's developing characters. Women who are situated along more unconventional socio-political and familial routes, queer identified Black mothers for example, are also likely to engage with Hip-Hop as a facet of their own as well as their children's worlds. In other cases, as with urban literature reading groups, the Hip-Hop sensibility is a vehicle for important cross-generational discussions about gendered identity, girlhood and womanhood for mothers, other-mothers, daughters and young women.

In this context of active daily interaction and practice, the deafening silence of women's voices and narrations on the matter of mothering in the context of Hip-Hop culture is striking. By contrast, male Hip-Hop artists, rappers in particular, have certainly taken the opportunity to pronounce on the subject: in their odes to mama, the berating of the lowly "baby-mama," and the romantic serenades to the potential "wifey." It is important to note that such popular representations are often constructed

1

and/or replicated in the larger context of an American social and political culture in which the peddling of gendered, racialized and highly limited representations of Black women and men has a long history. This collection, which is a compilation of critical essays, experiential reflections and interviews from a diversity of contributors including academics, community workers, activists and artists, is a step towards more frequent and expanded collective dialogues on mothering in Hip-Hop.

As an experience that is ever-present yet seemingly invisible in the now global music genre of Hip-Hop, motherhood has garnered little attention from journalists, writers and scholars of Hip-Hop culture. We have little understanding of how mothers who remain Hip-Hop enthusiasts negotiate their relationship to the culture of Hip-Hop and its music with their children. (Henry, Calixte and Knight, and Mouzon and Miller in this collection provide some insight into this dynamic.) Nor can we, with the exception of general critiques of representations of Black women in Hip-Hop, refer to a body of literature that illuminates the discursive spaces that motherhood occupies in Hip-Hop culture. (See Gosa, Powers, Nielson and Gumbs in this collection.) We have little guidance in pondering the role and position of mothering in Hip-Hop from a historical perspective (Campbell and I inch towards this in this collection), or the ways in which narrations of motherhood and mothering by women might trouble the hyper-masculinity and male-centredness that so overwhelmingly shape Hip-Hop's discursive and aesthetic practices (See Gumbs in this collection). Yvonne Bynoe's edited anthology, *Who's Your Mama? The Unsung Voices of Women and Mothers* (2009), touches the margins of the core thematic here. The aim of Bynoe's collection of mothers' personal narratives is to reveal and give voice to the diversity of mothering experiences against a dominant American motherhood discourse that takes white, well-educated, middle-class, and married heterosexual women as its standard. Though there are two pieces in Bynoe's edited collection written by women who work in the realm of Hip-Hop culture, the writers in question provide no commentary on their mothering experiences in the context of or in relation to this culture—an understandable (though telling) omission since Bynoe's collection carries the primary aim of more generally making visible the plurality of mothering styles and lives in America.

We may fortunately avail ourselves of a body of literature that provides anti-racist, feminist and class oriented critiques of Hip-Hop. Tricia Rose's *Black Noise* (1994) takes a seminal look at the artistic, social,

2

cultural and political configurations of Hip-Hop culture in America. Joan Morgan's *When Chickenheads Come Home to Roost* (2000) is a compelling analysis of Black women's love of Hip-Hop music; of sexism in Hip-Hop; of the ways in which women reinforce harmful and sexist stereotypes within Hip-Hop culture; and of the value of Hip-Hop as an important cultural resource in Black communities. Gwendolyn Pough's *Check It While I Wreck It* (2004) and *Home Girls Make Some Noise!* (2007), offer a genealogy of women's participation in American Hip-Hop, as well as a critical analysis of cultural representations of Black womanhood. Importantly, Pough's books examine rap as a feminist-inclined form of self-representation for women, and analyze the culture of sexism in Hip-Hop and American culture more widely. Patricia Hill Collins has also contributed a significant cultural critique in *From Black Power to Hip Hop* (2006), which forwards a feminist analysis of race, gender and national identity in the U.S. T. Denean Sharpley-Whiting's *Pimps Up, Ho's Down* (2008) and Ruth Nicole Brown's *Black Girlhood Celebration* (2008) make their own imprints on gender oriented Hip-Hop scholarship through their critique of misogyny in commercial Hip-Hop culture, the analysis of the elements that draw young women to demeaning dynamics in Hip-Hop, and the examination of the ways in which popular culture influences identity formation in girlhood. Notwithstanding these and other important contributions to the study of gender and power in Hip-Hop, one is hard pressed to find reflections, academic or otherwise, that focus on mothering as a vital component of Hip-Hop culture. For the diligent researcher, there are small morsels of information and clues now and then: a sentence or two buried in a magazine article, a passing comment in the run of an interview.

Motherhood has been a factor at play in the careers of a number of North America's prominent women Hip-Hop artists. Roxanne Shanté, widely recognized as the queen of battle rap, was a fourteen-year-old teenaged mother in 1984 when she was discovered by established rap producer Marlon "Marley Marl" Williams in the Queensbridge projects (Lushradioonline). Quoting Roxanne Shanté's rival at the time (The Real Roxanne) on motherhood in a 1990 interview with *Rappin'* magazine, Hip-Hop scholar Murray Forman notes this artist's refusal to hide her daughter away in the context of her music career, and the inspiration she drew from her child to continue with her education and get work. Murray insightfully suggests that The Real Roxanne's proud commitment to her daughter reflects "the way in which a female rapper's life and social conditions are entwined with her art, illustrating that Rap can help to focus one's perceptions and strengthen the understanding of a range of contradictory or complex experiences." Salt-N-Pepa have also juggled motherhood and music, acknowledging the challenges of mothering as a central component of their artistic lives. All three members of Salt-N-Pepa were single mothers who toured with their children during the most active periods of their careers ("Salt-N-Pepa Talk About the Things"). Unfortunately, the artists have seldom been asked to reflect on the role that this experience had on their development as artists and on their creative contributions to Hip-Hop communities. M.I.A. protégé Rye Rye, was newly signed to N.E.E.T./Interscope Records when, at eighteen, she became a mother (Cole). She had feared telling both M.I.A. and the record company of her pregnancy, underestimating the understanding she would garner from both, as well as the support she would receive from immediate family with childcare. Facing certain delay on her anticipated debut album, the now successful artist had initially resigned herself to career failure ("Rye Rye on Motherhood"). The mentorship of fellow mother and artist M.I.A. significantly influenced the negotiation that Rye Rye was able to make in juggling motherhood and a music career.

In reflecting on these factors and the ways in which we might critically assess the role of mothering in the context of Hip-Hop culture, this collection is theoretically framed by two interdisciplinary fields of study, feminist maternal theory and Hip-Hop studies. Feminist maternal theory explores motherhood as an institution, a set of systematized social expectations and modes of representation. This body of literature also examines the experience of mothering (e.g. Rich). The varied experience of mothering (the details of the *doing*) serves as the foundation of a theoretical framework and vocabulary (O'Reilly 3) that gives maternal theory its distinct academic characteristics. Sara Ruddick, in particular, is credited with the first extensively articulated scholarly examinations of *maternal thinking*——the theory produced out of the experience of mothering and in relation to the history of motherhood as an institution and identity (O'Reilly 3). Ruddick identifies a "discipline of maternal thought" (Ruddick 24) complete with a set of metaphysical attitudes, values and even methodologies (e.g. the act of judging between suitable pursuits) which are diversely observable in the practices of those who mother. Her re-conceptualization of mothering in the late 1980s, as a pursuit of choice rather than one inherent in a particular biology or gender, was a radical theoretical contribution to the area of motherhood studies (O'Reilly) and feminist theory. This intellectual line of exploration has bearing on and is augmented, for instance, in Alexis Pauline Gumbs' chapter in this collection. Gumbs unsettles racist and patriarchal representations of motherhood in America, along with sexist and problematic equivalents in Hip-Hop culture, by examining Black mothering as a queered subversive practice in a hostile national context, and as a practice that innovatively transcends masculine/feminine binaries.

Mothering, *mother-work* (the exercise of "protection, nurturance, and training" of the young (O'Reilly 2), and the institution of motherhood are examined in this collection in the context of Hip-Hop *culture*, where culture is taken to mean a vibrant, evolving set of shared beliefs, practices, attitudes and values that are given organized existential expression in a given historical period. The field of Hip-Hop studies has examined Hip-Hop as a cultural phenomenon framed by unique musical, linguistic, discursive, and artistic practices; as "a way of life" and a significant site of identity formation, expression and contestation (Alim and Pennycook 90/93). Gender-based analysis in Hip-Hop studies has, generally, focused on a set of key themes: the historical presence and participation of women in Hip-Hop culture; the negative representation of Black women in commercial Hip-Hop; the sexual objectification of women and the racialized methods used to do this (video vixens; exoticizing light/tanned skin); the misogyny that runs rampant in rap music; the means by which agency and empowerment are evident in some women artists' self-representation; and how girls and women's participation is situated in and contributes to Hip-Hop culture, though this is by no means an exhaustive list.

Representations of motherhood in Hip-Hop culture, for their part, have congealed around Black damage imagery (Powers), dating back to the American plantation slavery system. This set of representations place Black women along a limited image framework in which mothers are either versions of the perpetually self-sacrificing (and respectable) Strongblackwoman or a version of the disreputed Jezebel (lascivious and lewd). Oftentimes, the Monstrous/Evil Black Mother construction draws on elements of both of the aforementioned archetypes, representing pathology of overbearing (even violent) strength and deviant sexuality. In American commercial rap music, the Strongblackwoman, the Wifey and the Baby-Mama archetypes dominate representations

5

of motherhood that themselves resonate in a larger national social context which is over-determined by an idealized model of the White, middle-class, privatized, heterosexual nuclear family. This familial model is staunchly promulgated and defended as *the* "normal" family design through un-abating patriarchal ideologies of the family, despite the fact that (or perhaps precisely because) it has been on the wane, with family structure increasingly characterized by a diversity of formations that continue to be the source of nurturance, love and stability for many North Americans.

Black women have long struggled with social and political manifestations of the institution of motherhood in the context of a racist and patriarchal American national culture. By contemporary terms, this national cultural context is one in which Black women are meant to strive for heterosexual respectability, no better epitomized than by "Mom in Chief" Michelle Obama (pious, well-educated, domestically oriented, sexually reserved, and comfortable assuming a supportive/secondary/complementary spousal role, Young 33). Failing this, Black women risk hyperbolic chastisement and placement somewhere along the slippery slope to pathological monstrosity. This trend of binary, limiting and often offensive representations matters experientially. It produces a tension between the diversity of ways in which Black women understand, define and experience motherhood (Collins 1990), and the gross reductionism evident in representations that are produced within the realm of the American popular imagination. The following sections describe the thematic structuring of *Mothering in Hip-Hop Culture* according to two overarching considerations: cultural representations of motherhood and experiences of mothering in the context of Hip-Hop culture.

REPRESENTATION

In this section, Travis Gosa, Nicholas Powers, Erik Nielson and Alexis Pauline Gumbs assess practices of representation from several vantage points: the ways in which male rappers' odes to their mothers discursively unsettle the ideology of motherhood in America; the Mother/Whore dichotomy in Hip-Hop as symptomatic of male hysteria; rappers' representations of (their mothers') mothering practices as a key element of life-long community-based identity formation; and Black motherhood, in the example of MeShell Ndegeocello, as an epistemic standpoint that provides important openings through which parenting and maternal practices may be queered and radicalized.

Gosa critically examines what, by American standards, constitutes a good mother, and troubles the criteria on which these standards rely by turning our attention to the contestation that has always surrounded them. In America, good motherhood, he points out, has been grounded in the norms of White heteronormative bourgeois patriarchy. Good (future) mothers are expected to follow a respectable path to motherhood. They attain a certain level of education so as to be good prospective mates to a man and good future guardians of children; they get married to a man; and then become mothers who prioritize their family and household above career and other ambitions. In addition to following the path of heteronormative respectability and attaining or angling for middle-class socio-economic standing, the culmination of the good mother's achievement rests in the ultimate status attainment of her children. Gosa focuses on the ways in which male rappers turn a hegemonic model of motherhood on its head, offering an alternative mothering discourse by which Black children affirm their mothers in the context of a society that disparages and often reviles Black motherhood (Collins 1990: 137).

Gosa notes that the tributes of male rappers to their mothers often emphasize and positively detail mother-work. Rather than reading their mothers according to dominant norms framing the racist institution of motherhood in America, these rappers focus on the daily *doing* of mothering, and the ways in which their mothers succeeded in being there for them. The function of such an analysis is to flip the ideology of good motherhood to allow for different understandings of what makes a good mother, based on attention to the details of mothering rather than the extent to which a woman fits the institution of (good) motherhood. In Gosa's chapter, we see that rappers, including Brand Nubian, Can-I-Bus, Ghostface Killah, Jay-Z, Kanye West, Nas, Snoop Dogg, Talib Kweli, and Tupac Shakur, accent the love, efforts and presence of their mothers over the course of their lives, over and above any particular social status their mothers or they themselves may have been able to attain. Importantly, Gosa also cautions that the capacity of rap to unsettle the dominant ideology of motherhood in America is complicated by the rampant sexism and misogynistic rhetoric in much of the music. The subversive discursive potential of mother tributes in rap is, therefore, curtailed by the fact that rappers can wax poetic about their mothers on one track, and rap about raping and killing other people's mothers on another. As Gosa insightfully points out, "rappers love their mothers, but do not love all mothers." Interestingly, Erik Nielson (in this volume) to whose chapter I will turn attention further on in this introduction, remarks (in line with an observation made by Patricia Hill Collins), that Black men can praise their mothers while refusing accountability to the mothers of their own children (Collins 1990: 116). Nielson notes that mother tributes in rap reflect the positive centrality of Black matriarchs to their children's existential musings on authenticity and origin, as well as to the extended family and women-centred networks that sustain and nurture Black communities (Collins 1990).

In the second chapter, Nicholas Powers presents the Madonna/Slut binary as a psychological complex—as he terms it, the Mother/Whore complex—and more compellingly, demonstrates male rapper Jay-Z as exemplary of a particular type of African-American male hysteria. Powers sketches masculine hysteria as a form of self-medication for the emotionally wounded male rapper. Powers' chapter prods readers to move beyond simply observing and critiquing the myriad forms of misrepresentation at work in the rhetoric and aesthetics of commercial Hip-Hop and rap storytelling. He, additionally, proposes a psychoanalytic explanation for the fundamental purpose that such imagined worlds serve for the male artists who are invested in fashioning them. Powers relies on a combination of Marxist influenced philosophy (Althusser) and psychoanalytic theory (Freudian, Lacanian) to forward a persuasive analysis of the complex underlying dynamics that frame what often appears to be a love/hate relationship between men and women in Hip-Hop.

Erik Nielson considers the positive representations of mothering practices overwhelmingly forwarded by male rappers as constituting a narrative quilt detailing communities in which women as mothers occupy central roles of authority, guardianship and sustenance. Nielson views the dichotomy between the mother on a pedestal and the denigration of women more broadly in rap, as revealing interesting fissures in which male rappers—in acknowledging the significant contributions of their mothers in their lives—also provide evidence for the pivotal contribution of women to Black communities and rap and Hip-Hop culture more broadly. Rappers do this, in part, by absenting fathers in their music, making little mention of them in their songs, and congruently, masculinising the mothers they praise, "either by explicitly equating them to fathers, or by attributing to them characteristics reserved for men." Nielson points out a gender role reversal, in which mothers are commended in mother tracks for Herculean child rearing efforts under conditions of great struggle, often as sole providers with little or no help from the fathers of their children. This praise is an attempt to positively represent Black mothers in their grit and strength, but can also be seen to reflect the rappers' subtle absorption of more widely circulating negative representations of Black mothers in which women-headed households are discussed in the context of lack and deficiency. As Alexis Pauline Gumbs indicates (in this volume) Hip-Hop artists do often share stories in which their mothers are characterized as acting as both mother and father, but these stories, unfortunately, do not escape some of the negative connotations frequently associated with the "single mother" household. Familial completeness is seldom attributed to this type of household, which is dogged by the focus on lack (framed by the assumed absence of male figures from the child's life). Rappers, in paying tribute to the determined and pimp-like (Powers, Chapter 2) efforts of their mothers, importantly recognize the mother-work of these women and flip the normative American script on motherhood; but they also, perhaps unintentionally, reinforce a hyperbolic and racialized discourse of fatherlessness, through which we are to understand the mothers' efforts and activities as (by necessity) prompted by the very absence or ineffectiveness of Black men as fathers. Understandably, "glorifying the strong Black mother represents Black men's attempts to replace negative white male interpretations with positive Black male ones" (Collins 1990: 117). However, as genuine as these efforts may be, they have frequently contributed to a roster of circulating tropes surrounding Black womanhood that Black feminists have long critiqued (e.g. hooks; Roberts; Wallace).

Black mothers and their roles in Black communities have historically been pathologized in institutions and scholarship relying on white supremacist and heteropatriarchal ideology (e.g. Moynihan report of 1965, *The Negro Family: The Case for National Action*). By contrast, tributes to mothers in rap focus on a mother's love. Where Moynihan saw pathology, many rappers see resolve, creativity and devotion. This is a love that is apparent in the detailed accounting by rappers of the ways their mothers nurtured and protected them; the ways they were given care and comforted while sick, the special efforts their mothers made to prepare their favourite foods (an act that is represented as providing not only physical but also spiritual nourishment), the efforts made to keep them in school and out of trouble, and the formative musical influences that their mothers shared with them. This last point is especially significant, Nielson points out, since it not only affirms the positive roles of mothers in Black communities, but also indicates their influence on the musical formation of their sons. The subjects of Nielson's analysis represent the diversity of family experience and the ambition of rappers (in this case the narrators of these experiences) to positively impact the familial sites of the maternal love they experienced as children. While the mothers in these songs occupy a privileged and exceptional space in the rap genre as a whole (mothers-to-be in the form of "wifeys," and baby-mammas are generally exempt from such honour), and the omissions this reflects is certainly important to critical assessments of the discursive utility of mother tracks to empowering visions of motherhood, Nielson indicates that the tracks, nonetheless, exhibit the positive centrality of women in the community-based identity formation that is at the core of rappers' existential ruminations about their own origins and destiny.

Alexis Pauline Gumbs reflects on the contributions of Black feminist mothering to Hip-Hop culture. Referring to the work of musician MeShell Ndegeocello, and relying theoretically on the writings of Audre Lorde, Gumbs takes readers from the counter-productive "slandering of mothers (in the "your mama" tradition), the criminalization of baby mamas as gold-diggers and the debasement of women's sexuality and reproductive agency in general" in rap and Hip-Hop culture—to a "body of work [that] reminds us that Hip-Hop can also be a queer dialogical space where the meaning of parenting is up for grabs." For Gumbs, Black mothering can in many ways already be read as a queer practice—that is, a queering of the status quo. She argues that Black mothering may be viewed as queer in the context of a dominant narrative in the U.S. that has and continues to construct Black motherhood as unnatural, prone to deviancy, and responsible for decreasing the life chances of its offspring and charges (Gumbs). Gumbs' queer lens exceeds the usual scope of gay, lesbian and queer studies, which she critiques elsewhere for a white-centredness and tendency to neglect or portray mothering as though it is "the least radical thing one can do" (Gumbs). Drawing on the concept of "shine" in Hip-Hop lexicon (focussing on its use in matters concerning capitalist accumulation and Black self-love/self-actualization), Gumbs explores queer Black mothering as a means to affirm Black life and transform the meaning of parenting. What might it mean to think of a mothering in which, instead of being shamed, guilt-tripped and pushed into yearning for a patriarch as *the* route to familial health, (Black) women could (à la MeShell Ndegeocello) conceive of *themselves* as the man of their dreams, and affirm themselves for the ways in which they embody parental abundance? We have examples of visions to strengthen Black communities that depend on proposals to return Black men to their "rightful" patriarchal roles in Black households. Drawing from Audre Lorde, Gumbs contends that the mother-son relationship as sanctioned by dominant cultural norms and reproduced in culturally specific ways in the context of Hip-Hop culture, is un-healthy. It is a relationship model that outsources the labour of feeling to women, feminizes empathy, and encourages emotional repression in men, producing manifestations of hyper-masculinity that are counterproductive to life affirming collective practices in Black communities. Gumbs' analysis provocatively queers the subject, using Ndegeocello's musicality and its relationship to Hip-Hop as a means of both "revaluing undervalued social practices" and opening out modes of Black parenting.

EXPERIENCE

In the second section of this collection, Shana Calixte, Ruth Henry, Shantelena Mouzon and Sharon Miller, and Mark Campbell and myself provide a glimpse into the day-to-day lives of women artists balancing and negotiating their art and professions with motherhood. Calixte interviews the dynamic Eekwol of the Muskoday First Nation on her recent projects, her experiences within the Canadian music industry, and the negotiations these require of her as a mother. Henry (MC Oasis) takes us on several journeys between Boston and various parts of Colombia, as she connects with organic Hip-Hop communities in Cartagena and returns to the U.S. to mentor young people through her creativity and artistic abilities. We are drawn to the transnational connections between the socio-economic challenges facing Black youth in Boston and the political dynamics framing the war related struggles of communities in Colombia. As stories and letters cross national borders through Henry, we are led to identify the cultural multiplicities that inform this artist's political awareness and artistic commitment. That her children accompany her and are made active participants in this journey makes Henry's narrative all the more interesting.

Mouzon (Helixx C. Armageddon) and Miller (Pri The Honey Dark) are artists based in Queens, New York. They are members of all-woman Hip-Hop collective Anomolies, founded in 1995 as a means of pro-actively creating spaces for women to, among other aims, develop their careers in Hip-Hop in a context of personal and professional integrity. The Anomolies crew, comprised of Emcees, DJs, b-girls, producers and visual artists, has performed throughout the United States, opening for MC Lyte, Talib Kweli and Bahamadia, among others. They remain active in Hip-Hop culture through participation in Hip-Hop festivals and workshops, and their nurturing of links to schools and community organizations.[1] For this volume, Anomolies core members Mouzon and Miller, both mothers, sit for a conversation on their artistic achievements and the challenges and rewards of mothering in Hip-Hop communities.

The final experiential chapter of this volume features interviews with two notable women artists in Canadian Hip-Hop. Lady P was arguably Canada's first woman Emcee, paving the way for renowned artist Michie Mee and others. DJ Mel Boogie has built an impressive place for herself in the Canadian Hip-Hop circuit, leading Canada's only all-woman Hip-Hop radio show and stacking an impressive roster of performances at concerts, clubs and other events. This chapter examines the artists' narratives on their early beginnings in Hip-Hop, and their experiences as women and mothers in the industry. The authors note the recurrence of the theme of sacrifices made to motherhood, successes gained despite the challenges of motherhood, and the importance of family support in the development of their music careers.

CONCLUDING COMMENTS

Since its emergence in the South Bronx during the late 1970s, Hip-Hop has attained global reach, inspiring a diversity of localized appropriations in regions around the world. Hip-Hop music is at home in Europe, Latin America, the Caribbean, Africa, Asia, the Pacific, and the Middle East—in musical genres as diverse as Bhangra, Kwaito, Rock, Salsa and Soukous. Women, of course, have had a significant hand in sustaining Hip-Hop culture all over the world. Yet, little is known of their involvement in Hip-Hop outside of North America and a few European regions. More generally, even less is understood about motherhood as a dimension of women's experiences as rappers, dancers, filmmakers, producers, DJs, graphic artists, music enthusiasts, and writers/narrators of Hip-Hop culture. When Tamil-British rapper M.I.A. performed at the 2009 Grammy Awards while nine months pregnant, she appeared on stage alongside some of rap's best known contemporary male front-liners: T.I., Lil Wayne, Jay Z and Kanye West. Ensuing coverage of the event stated the obvious—that she was *very* pregnant. Yet no writers or interviewers before or after this particular event made any attempt to grapple with the explicitly radical interjections her body and presence were making in the usual Hip-Hop refrain, one personified so well in the work of the men with whom she shared the stage that evening. The shock waves running through online networks following M.I.A.'s Grammy performance centred on delivering judgment on whether or not it was appropriate for a woman *that* pregnant, and in such a revealing dress, to be out and about, rocking and shaking it with the big boys. Outrage at the extent to which her pregnancy was visible, evident in comments ranging from "M.I.A. is hella pregeant [sic],"[2] "She looked a hot mess,"[3] "I ain't been right since!"[4] and "This is the longest that 4 black guys hung around a pregnant chick,"[5] illustrate both the normative silence and strategic referencing reserved for motherhood in Hip-Hop, as well as the interplay between racial reasoning and sexuality in gender tropes. Given this public atmosphere, M.I.A.'s (and other artist mothers'—Lauryn Hill, Erykah Badu) rapping, dancing and claim of a vocal public presence while bearing the literal mark of motherhood occupies an obvious but under-theorized aspect of cultural production.

This collection aims to give motherhood within Hip-Hop culture an intellectual point of entry into an existing field of academic debates that have largely focused on analyzing the sexual objectification of women, the valorisation of violent masculinity, fierce homophobia and rampant consumerism in Hip-Hop. The focus is on an obvious yet neglected reality: mothers are artists in Hip-Hop culture; they claim ownership over the process of cultural production in this domain; they have particular ways of understanding their mothering experiences in the context of artistic practice, as well as the implications of these experiences for Hip-Hop culture. The book is a modest but important step. It draws on the sparse literature available on this subject, and the creativity and efforts of its contributors to pull together beginning elements of a crucial conversation.

A heartfelt thank you goes out to the two anonymous reviewers of this manuscript, whose incisive and well-placed comments served to strengthen the articulation of the collection's aims. Any shortcomings thereafter are entirely my own.

[1] Anomolies Crew. *MySpace* page. Web. <http://www.myspace.com/anomolies>.
[2] <http://www.youtube.com/watch?v=mB7AY4qt-HQ&feature=related>.
[3] <http://answers.yahoo.com/question/index?quid=20090208185826AAR4hDq>.
[4] Ibid.
[5] <http://dailycontributor.com/video-very-pregnant-mia-performs-at-the-grammys/33991>.

WORKS CITED

Alim, H. Samy and Alastair Pennycook. "Glocal Linguistic Flows: Hip-Hop Culture(s), Identities, and the Politics of Language Education." *Journal of Language, Identity, and Education* 6.2 (2007): 89-100.

Brown, Ruth Nicole. *Black Girlhood Celebration*. New York: Peter Lang Publishing, 2008.

Bynoe, Yvonne. *Who's Your Mama? The Unsung Voices of Women and Mothers*. New York: Soft Skull Press, 2009.

Collins, Patricia Hill. *From Black Power to Hip Hop: Racism, Nationalism, and Feminism*. Philadelphia: Temple University Press, 2006.

Collins, Patricia Hill. *Black Feminist Thought: Knowledge, Consciousness, and the Politics of Empowerment*. New York: Routledge, 1990.

Forman, Murray. "'Movin' Closer to an Independent Funk': Black Feminist Theory, Standpoint, and Women in Rap." *Women's Studies* 23 (1994): 35-55.

Gumbs, Alexis Pauline. "Forget Hallmark: Why Mother's Day is a Queer Black Left Feminist Thing." NewBlackMan (online blog), Thursday, May 7, 2009. Web. <http://newblackman.blogspot.com/2009/05/forget-hallmark-why-mothers-day-is.html>.

hooks, bell. *Reel to Real: Race, Sex, and Class at the Movies*. New York: Routledge, 1996.

Lushradioonline. "Exclusive Interview W/ the Mother of Hip-Hop Dr. Roxanne Shante Along with Special Guests." *Blogtalkradio*. 19 June 2009.

Web. <http://www.blogtalkradio.com/lushradioonline/2009/06/19/exclusive-interview-wthe-mother-of-hip-hop-drroxanne-shante-along-with-special-guests>.

Morgan, Joan. *When Chickenheads Come Home to Roost: A Hip-Hop Feminist Breaks it Down*. New York: Simon & Schuster, 2000.

Moynihan, Daniel Patrick. *The Negro Family: The Case for National Action*. Washington, DC: Office of Policy Planning and Research, U.S. Department of Labor, 1965.

O'Reilly Andrea, ed. *Maternal Thinking: Philosophy, Politics, Practice*. Bradford: Demeter Press, 2009.

Pough, Gwendolyn D. *Check it While I Wreck it: Black Womanhood, Hip-Hop Culture, and the Public Sphere*. Boston: Northeastern University Press, 2004.

Pough, Gwendolyn D., ed. *Home Girls Make Some Noise! Hip-Hop Feminism Anthology*. Mira Loma: Parker Publishing Inc., 2007.

Powers, Nicholas. " 'Precious' or How I Learned to Stop Worrying and Love the Movie." *The Indypendent*, December 8, 2009. Web. <http://www.indypendent.org/2009/12/08/precious-or-how-i-learned-stop-worrying-and-love-movie>.

Rachel, T. Cole. "Hip-Hop's Latest It Girl: Rye Rye." *Details.com*. February 2011. Web. <http://www.details.com/celebrities-entertainment/music-and-books/201102/rye-rye-hip-hop-music-artist-interview>.

Rich, Adrienne. *Of Woman Born: Motherhood as Experience and Institution*. New York: Norton, 1976.

Roberts, Dorothy E. "The Value of Black Mothers' Work." *Connecticut Law Review* 26 (1993-1994): 871-878.

Rose, Tricia. *Black Noise: Rap Music and Black Culture in Contemporary America*. Hanover: Wesleyan University Press, 1994.

Ruddick, Sara. *Maternal Thinking: Toward a Politics of Peace*. Boston: Beacon Press, 1989.

"Rye Rye on Motherhood, Female Rap, and Nicki Minaj". *RapUpTV*. You Tube. 24 May 2010. Web. <http://www.youtube.com/watch?v=P-Gy3OunErKg&feature=relmfu>.

"Salt-N-Pepa Talk About the Things Men Need to be Taught." *Jet Magazine*. 1 December 1997: 56-60. Online: <http://books.google.com/books>.

Sharpley-Whiting, T. Denean. *Pimps Up, Ho's Down: Hip Hop's Hold on Young Black Women*. New York: New York University Press, 2007.

Wallace, Michele. *Black Macho and the Myth of the Superwoman*. New York: Verso, 1999.

Young, Courtney C. "Monstrous Mothering from *Boyz 'N' the Hood* to *Precious*: Damaged Mothers on Screen." *Illuminating the Dark Side: Evil, Women and the Feminine*. Eds. Andrea Ruthven and Gabriela Mádlo. Oxford: Inter-Disciplinary Press, 2010. 33-38.

1.

"Mama Tried"

Narratives of Good Mothering in Rap Music

TRAVIS L. GOSA

WHAT DOES IT MEAN to be a "good" mother? In the contemporary American context, mothering is rarely discussed outside of White, middle-class norms. The hegemonic model of motherhood dictates that women complete their education, enter into a heterosexual marital relationship, and then plan for motherhood (Edin and Kefalas 165).[1] After childbirth, women are pressured to prioritize the household, children, and husband's needs over their own career ambitions (Douglas and Michaels). In this paradigm, mother quality is measured by the status attainment of children. The children of good mothers are expected to do well at school, excel in both athletic competitions and the piano, gain admission to prestigious colleges, land white-collar jobs, get married, and eventually have children of their own (Hays; Rosenfield and Wise; Lareau).

This chapter explores how Hip-Hop culture, specifically rap music, provides an alternative mothering discourse. Mother-inspired rap anthems such as Tupac Shakur's "Dear Mama," Kanye West's "Hey Mama," and Nas' "Dance" have had considerable commercial success. It would seem that almost every major artist has dropped an "I-love-my-momma-esque" track. Rappers as diverse as Snoop Dogg ("I Love My Momma!"), Talib Kweli ("Mamma Can You Hear Me?"), Brand Nubian ("Momma"), Jay-Z ("Mama Loves Me"), Ghostface Killah ("All That I Got Is You"), and Can-I-Bus ("I Honor U") present odes to their mothers.[2] These songs often challenge established norms of mothering. According to rappers, urban-poor-single mothers can be good mothers in ways that do not require middle-class resources. The autobiographical stories told by rappers give voice to an alternative vision of mothering that privileges presence, effort, and love, rather than child outcomes.

By categorizing the discursive framing of mother tracks, I attempt to complicate portrayals of rap's gender politics as a one-dimensional celebration of hyper-masculine, woman-hating rhetoric. These songs represent fleeting moments in which male rappers reaffirm the value of Black women's labor power in the household by re-racing/re-classing notions of good mothering. A growing literature seeks to establish Hip-Hop's potential as a new feminist space (Morgan; Pough). This chapter continues this line of work by focusing on the gender politics located in narratives of non-romantic, familial relationships (Tyree).

To contextualize the discursive significance of mother-raps, I provide a brief review of hegemonic mothering ideology. In the second section, I explore some of the broad themes of rap's mothering discourse. Lyrics are used to develop a working definition of what is generally described as good mothering in Hip-Hop. The chapter concludes with a discussion of how rap's ability to disrupt dominant mothering ideology is complicated by the prominence of misogyny and anti-woman rhetoric. I argue that mother-raps construct protected categories for some women but do not represent an emancipatory narrative for all women.

MOTHERING AS IDEOLOGY IN ACTION

Presumably, all mothers regardless of circumstance want to be good mothers and provide the best for their children. Mothers who supply emotional support, encouragement, and structure create a sturdy foundation for their children's development (Elder et al.; Baumrind). But outside of widely condemned parental excesses (emotional, physical, psychological "abuses"), it remains difficult to identify any one approach to ideal mothering. What constitutes good and bad practices are a matter of family context and structural opportunity, not individual behavior (Baumrind; Pinderhughes et al.).

The meaning of mothering is a function of specific socio-historical ideology that is inseparable from geography, race-sex-gender norms, and social class interest. That is, what social norms deem as "good" or "bad" often functions to reinforce the interests of the powerful. As the literature on symbolic-interactionism indicates, power is maintained through symbolic meaning systems or ideologies (West and Zimmerman; Jackson). White, male, capitalist dominance is embedded in the rationality and hidden assumptions of American society that go deeper than discrimination or hate. Hegemonic ideology controls behavior and probable agency through discursive framing, the process of reducing the complexities of life into "common sense" stories (Berger and Quinney; Wuthnow). As Patricia Hill Collins observes, common sense provides the macro-micro link between systems of oppression and individual experience:

> To maintain their power, dominant groups create and maintain a popular system of 'common sense' ideas that support their right to rule. In the United States, hegemonic ideologies concerning race, class, gender, sexuality, and nation are often so pervasive that it is difficult to conceptualize alternatives to them, let alone ways of resisting the social practices that they justify. (284)

The popular mothering discourse has made it common sense that middle-class mothering styles are superior and necessary, while poor and Black mothers are portrayed as lazy, pathological, and even criminal (Kelley, Power, and Wimbush). Conversely, this discourse reinforces the myth of meritocracy by attributing the positive outcomes of middle-class children to superior mothering while obscuring unearned advantage (Johnson).

Hegemonic mothering hurts poor women, but it also places arbitrary limits on the lives of middle-class women. The dominant image of female success devalues motherhood by instructing women to consider childbirth only after consolidating middle-class status through college education, labor market success, and heterosexual marriage (Edin and Kefalas). After marriage, there is a slight shift in normative expectations as women are pressured to refocus on maintaining the needs of the households, children, and husband (Douglas and Michaels 5). Middle-class mothers are told to organize their daily lives around their children's endless quest for higher grades and niche extracurricular activities. But this often leaves super-mommies overburdened, exhausted, and in debt trying to achieve this image of perfect motherhood (Rosenfield and Wise). If and when relatively unsuccessful children are the result of this strategy, careerist mothers are also labeled bad mothers. Ironically, this feminine "failure" can connect her to the under-educated, under-employed mothers of whom she may have been judgmental. The "housewife-suburban-hockey-mom" model also tends to produce self-absorbed children who are hostile towards peers and siblings, spend little time with extended family, and possess a perverse sense of entitlement (Lareau).

NARRATIVES OF GOOD MOTHERING IN RAP MUSIC

The power of self-evident "truths" about mothering can be undermined by creating alternative discourses and maintaining spaces that operate on different logic systems. Rap music troubles the hegemonic conception of mothering by paying tribute to the mothering that is done by young (often teenage), poor, urban, minority, and unmarried women. Importantly, this alternative vision of good mothering emphasizes *mothering effort* over *child outcomes*. Good mothers simply "try" their best. Rap's archetype of mothering effort is comprised of three interlocking aspects of (a) presence, (b) effort, often in the form of struggle, and (c) unconditional love. Mothers who aspire to these characteristics are said to be good mothers even when these strategies result in raising boys who are killers, womanizers, and gangsters. These dynamics of good mothering are discussed in order.

"MAMA WAS ALWAYS THERE"

Mothers in the form of biological mothers, aunts, and (great-) grand-mothers ("big mammas") are prominent figures in rap songs because they are primarily responsible for the care and socialization of their sons. Unlike middle-class children, who tend to spend the majority of their time interacting with non-familial adults in structured activities, rappers recount how every aspect of their childhoods were controlled under the watchful eyes of single mothers. Scores of rappers relate in their autobiographical rhymes that a mother's constant presence provides reprieve from the pain of poverty and contempt of fatherlessness. Dedications to mothers usually contain harsh words for absent fathers. As the 1990s rap group Naughty By Nature famously declared on behalf of all "ghetto bastards," "I was one who never had and always mad/Never knew my dad, motherfuck the fag!"[3]

Unlike deadbeat dads, good mothers maintain both physical and emotional bonds with their children. Single mothers are said to provide the emotional support of a mother *and* father, a best friend, role model, and teacher in the absence of adult men. For example, Mike Jones explains that his deceased grandmother was his best friend but also provided discipline: "Grandma, remember when we used to play them bones [dominoes] and you would skunk us [game of tag]/And you never had a problem punkin' [disciplining] us in front of company." Jones says that his grandmother was the only person who believed that he could succeed in life. According to the story, his grandmother even created his trademark refrain of yelling his real name ("Mike Jones!") instead of a rap alias. "A lot of people always used to wonder how I got up in the game [became successful in the music industry]/ Y'knahmsayin? My grandma was 99.9 percent of the reason y'knahmsayin?" (MC Eiht).

As Erik Neilson explains in Chapter 3, mothers function as the "primary role models after which rappers pattern themselves, permitting them a level of reverence that is withheld from most other women." Mother tributes explain that good mothers never stop fulfilling the role of friend, inspiration, and creative manager. The resources of middle-class family life can buy access to music executives or formal music training. But, according to rappers like Mike Jones, a mother's wisdom and support can trump any of these material resources.

One of the ironies of hegemonic mothering is that children often come last—after the workday, or after playing the perfect wife at country-club parties. Hip-Hop's alternative discourse suggests that good mothers always prioritize the needs of children over status attainment. In many cases, "always being there" means putting the mother-son relationship ahead of romantic relationships with men. This can be seen in Lil' Wayne's "Word of Fantasy," a gripping story about his mother Jacita "Cita" Carter:

> Mama named Cita, I love You Cita
> [Re]Member when your pussy second husband used to beat ya?
> Remember when I went into the kitchen got the cleaver [knife]?
> He ain't give a fuck, I ain't give a fuck neither

On the track, Lil' Wayne recounts the abuse both he and his mother faced at the hands of a heroin-addicted stepfather. Fearing the loss of his mother, Lil' Wayne threatens the man with a knife, swearing that he would rather die than sever the bond with his mother. Because she stayed by his side instead of chasing drugs with her husband, Lil' Wayne explains that he is indebted forever to his mother. Good mothers stay committed to doing their best to raise their children despite poverty, fatherless, and drugs. Only bad mothers choose romantic relationships or drugs over their sons.

"MAMA TRIED"

Hip-Hop motherhood is idealized by the notion of struggle. While mainstream beliefs might suggest that having children without financial resources, fathers, and security is irresponsible, rappers describe this as nothing less than a heroic feat worthy of praise. According to the songs, real mothers fight against the odds of everyday life in the 'hood. Middle-class families take for granted food and shelter. But for poor mothers, providing the basics requires working multiple service industry positions, such as housekeeping or waitressing, all while attending community college and caring for children.

The struggle to provide material resources is important, but the hardest task may be keeping their sons on a positive developmental path. The good mothers described in rap try everything to keep their sons in school, church, and athletic activities, but they usually fail. Lyrics to "Hold Up" by MC Eiht provide an extended example of songs that detail the Herculean, but failed efforts of single mothers to raise their sons "right."

According to MC Eiht, his mother tried everything to keep him off the streets:

"Get A's in school
Keep your head up high and don't run with the fools"
That was the lesson, always listen to moms
Bible she totin', always quotin' from Psalms

Out of respect, MC Eiht pretends to listen, but says he like other Black boys, don't care about education or religion. By the second verse, MC Eiht is skipping school, selling drugs, and hanging with big hommies. These narratives usually suggest that good mothers struggle against the allure of the streets, but cannot provide the male companionship and modeling necessary to become a "real" man.

"UNCONDITIONAL LOVE FOR BAD BOYS"

Self-proclaimed "bad boys" eventually become the young men involved with violent street crime, absent-fatherhood, and the criminal justice system. According to the lyrics, good mothers continue to provide unconditional love for their adult children. That is, they stick by their children through the hard times and never give up hope that their sons are good at heart. Unlike affluent mothers, they do not disown their children for picking the wrong college major or career. The theme of unconditional love is demonstrated through tales of mothers who appear in the front row of the courtroom when their sons are sentenced to prison, and visit them regularly in prison.

The heartfelt songs that celebrate mothers are often apologies for bad boy behavior in the past. Rappers say that they are aware that their behavior caused a great deal of pain. As reparations, they promise to reward mothers for never giving up. This typically involves stories of lavishing mothers with expensive consumer goods. Apologies sometimes involve promises to shape up—as Kanye West promises his mother that he will go back to school—but these non-material claims sound empty in comparison to his plans to buy his mother a mansion, a "Benzo" [Mercedes Benz] with tinted windows, a "S-Type" Jaguar sports car, and "upper-echelon" restaurants ("Hey Mama").

The expectation of and repayment for a mother's love is significant given the tone of male-female relationships envisioned by rap music. The idea of an unconditional love between mothers and sons is given so much meaning because most male-female interactions are said not to involve love. In the "Pimp-Hoe" archetype, fear and violence are used to control women's behavior, while the "Bonnie-N'-Clyde" coupling is conditional on the woman's ability to "ride or die" for her man. In the most conditional relationship, the "Playa-Bitch" dynamic can be dissolved when a man gets tired or bored with the sex—he is then free to pass the woman to the rest of his friends.

Rap's discussion of mothers can unsettle the stereotype of the lazy, self-absorbed welfare queen. In this sense, rappers should be commended for reminding the world about the value of mothering in forms that do not fit the normative framework. However, there are real boundaries to the emancipatory narrative presented here. Primarily, rappers are creating motherhood as a semi-protected category for some women (e.g., their mothers), while further subjugating most women. The celebration of one's own mother is not extended to motherhood or women in general. Rappers present tearful prose to their mothers in one verse, while threatening to rape and kill everyone else's mother on the next track. Lil' Wayne's exposition of how he will treat *your* grandmother and the mother of *your* children provides a succinct example of this contradiction:

> I might crazy go on these niggas, I don't give a motherfuck
> Run up in a nigga house and shoot his grandmother up, what!
> What, I don't give a motherfuck, get cha baby kidnapped
> And ya baby's mother fucked. ("3 Peat")

Rappers love their mothers, but do not love all mothers.[4]

Likewise, rappers continue to refer to most women as disposable bitches, skeezers, tricks, hoes, chickenheads, and jump-offs. This tendency can be heard on the track "Hate It Or Love It," in which The Game and 50 Cent pay homage to the memories of their deceased grandmother and mother (respectively), but in the same verse threaten to kill and/or fuck your daughter for a small fee. Male rappers routinely label their "baby mamas" as "gold diggers" who get pregnant for the sole purpose of receiving child support payments.

Hip-Hop is counter-culture, to be sure. But it is also popular culture that reinforces the all-American "–ism's" of (hetero)sexism, materialism, and capitalism. The mom-songs discussed in this chapter should be read with the pretext that gender conflict, specifically the attempt to silence and exclude the participation, sensibilities, and the agency of women, has been central to the socio-historical project of masculinity *and* Hip-Hop. Hip-Hop has always been a male-centered, male-dominated enterprise created for the pleasure and self-esteem building of young men (see George; Morgan). Respected Hip-Hop journalist *Touré* provides a succinct description of the race-gender politics of Hip-Hop: "This world [Hip-Hop] was built to worship urban Black maleness: the way we speak, walk, dance, dress, think. We are revered by others, but our leadership is and will remain Black. As it should" (101).

Cultural practices that involve female empowerment present a radical threat to the worship of urban Black maleness, and therefore will be incomplete and fleeting at best. Thus, we will hear Kanye West produce an occasional "Hey Mama," but most songs will sound like "Gold Digger." The memory of Tupac Shakur will continue to be commemorated for pro-mother songs like "Dear Mama," "Keep Ya' Head Up," and "Brenda's Got A Baby," but we must not forget that most of his tracks sounded more like "All 'Bout You ("The Same Hoe") and "I Get Around."

A pessimistic interpretation of Hip-Hop might include dismissing these songs altogether. Many rappers are intelligent, savvy businessmen who are well aware that a strategically placed momma-song on an album can offset criticism of woman hating, or provide the one radio-friendly hit for airwaves. This is a plausible interpretation. But the perspective of Hip-Hop feminism touted by scholars like Tricia Rose, Marcyliena Morgan, Imani Perry, Eithne Quinn, Kyra Gaunt, Ruth Nichole Brown, Gwendolyn Pough, Kelli Goff, Joan Morgan, and Cheryl Keyes—and "traditional" feminist scholars such as Patricia Hill Collins and bell hooks—encourage us to maintain an empathetic yet critical gaze on Hip-Hop.[5] This means understanding the structural incentives that produce a market for rap songs about mother loving *and* woman-killing. Hip-Hop feminism also requires that we demand that rappers go beyond heartfelt songs about their mothers to attacking practices that preserve male privilege. If male rappers really want to demonstrate their love for mothers, a first step might include treating girlfriends with dignity, and being good fathers and role models to children. Unfortunately, few artists say that paying back mothers will include these changes in behavior.[6] Male rappers' mothering discourse succeeds in unsettling some of the tenets of the institution of motherhood, but does little to challenge gender norms.

[1]Mothering is typically imagined as individual women caring for their biological offspring. This also tends to ignore non-familial mothers ("aunties" and "play cousins") and grandmothers ("big mammas") who play important roles in the lives of children. Except when referring to "hegemonic mothering" or "middle-class mothering," the use of mothers in this essay should signal a broad, expanded conception of motherhood.
[2]I was able to download and listen to over 100 mother-centric rap songs. In this chapter, I limit my discussion to the themes provided by male artists without regard to time period or sub-genre categorization.
[3]The absence of fathers is an enduring theme in rap music. There are notable exceptions, as rappers Nas and Common, for example, have had their fathers perform music and songs on their albums. These celebrations of fathers still seem rare.
[4]The African-American tradition of "playing the dozens," "snapping,"

"capping," or "your mama jokes" involves a competition of quick-witted insults and wordplay meant to be humorous. In addition, Kyra Gaunt discusses the connection of "your mama" double-dutch chants recounted by girls to the early formation of Hip-Hop. These threats of violence against mothers do not appear to contain the same spirit of humor.

[5]This is by no means an exhaustive list or even the most influential in the field, but these are female authors who take an explicitly feminist view in their writings on Hip-Hop culture.

[6]Prominent exceptions would be Public Enemy's "Brother's Gonna Work It Out" and Outkast's "Ms. Jackson" in which they propose that black men should treat all women and children with respect.

WORKS CITED

Baumrind, Diana. "The Discipline Controversy Revisited." *Family Relations* 45.4 (1996): 405-14.

Berger, Ronald J., and Richard Quinney. *Storytelling Sociology: Narrative as Social Inquiry.* Boulder, Colo.: Lynne Rienner, 2005.

Collins, Patricia Hill. *Black Feminist Thought: Knowledge, Consciousness and the Politics of Empowerment.* 2nd ed. New York: Routledge, 2000.

Douglas, Susan Jeanne, and Meredith W. Michaels. *The Mommy Myth: The Idealization of Motherhood and How It Has Undermined All Women.* New York: Free Press, 2005.

Edin, Kathryn, and Maria Kefalas. *Promises I Can Keep: Why Poor Women Put Motherhood before Marriage.* Berkeley: University of California Press, 2005.

Elder, Glen H. Jr., Jacquelynne S. Eccles, Monika Ardelt and Sarah Lord. "Inner-City Parents under Economic Pressure: Perspectives on the Strategies of Parenting." *Journal of Marriage and the Family* 57.3 (1995): 771-84.

Gaunt, Kyra. *The Games Black Girls Play: Learning the Ropes from Double-Dutch to Hip-Hop.* New York: New York University Press, 2006.

George, Nelson. *Hip Hop America.* New York: Viking, 1998.

Hays, Sharon. *The Cultural Contradictions of Motherhood.* New Haven: Yale University Press, 1996.

Jackson, John L., Jr. *Harlemworld: Doing Race and Class in Contemporary Black America.* Chicago, Ill: London University of Chicago Press, 2001.

Johnson, Heather Beth. *The American Dream and the Power of Wealth:*

Choosing Schools and Inheriting Inequality in the Land of Opportunity. London: Routledge, 2006.

Kanye West. "Hey Mama." *Late Registration.* Roc-A-Fella/Island Def Jam, 2005.

Kelley, Michelle L., Thomas G. Power, and Dawn D. Wimbush. "Determinants of Disciplinary Practices in Lowincome Black Mothers." *Child Development* 63.3 (1992): 573-82.

Lareau, Annette. *Unequal Childhoods: Class, Race, and Family Life.* Berkeley: University of California Press, 2003.

Lil' Wayne. "Word of Fantasy." *The Drought Is Over 2, The Carter 3 Sessions.* The Empire, 2007.

Lil' Wayne. "3 Peat." *Tha Carter 3.* Cash Money/Universal/Young Money, 2008.

MC Eiht. "Hold Up." *N' My Neighborhood.* Hoo Bangin'/Priority, 2000.

Mike Jones. "Grandma." *Who Is Mike Jones?* Swisherhouse/Warner Bros., 2005.

Morgan, Joan. *When Chickenheads Come Home to Roost: My Life as a Hip-Hop Feminist.* New York: Simon & Schuster, 2000.

Naughty By Nature. "Everything's Gonna Be Alright (Ghetto Bastard). *Naughty By Nature.* Tommy Boy Records, 1991.

Pinderhughes, Ellen E., Robert Nix, E. Michael Foster and Damon Jones. "Parenting in Context: Impact of Neighborhood Poverty, Residential Stability, Public Services, Social Networks, and Danger on Parental Behaviors." *Journal of Marriage and the Family* 63.4 (2001): 941-53.

Pough, Gwendolyn. *Check it While I Wreck It: Black Womanhood, Hip-Hop Culture, and the Public Sphere.* Boston: Northeastern University Press, 2004.

Rosenfeld, Alvin A. and Nicole Wise. *The Over-Scheduled Child: Avoiding the Hyper-Parenting Trap.* 1st ed. New York: St. Martin's Griffin, 2001.

The Game feat. 50 Cent. "Hate It Or Love It." *The Documentary.* Aftermath/G-Unit/Interscope Records, 2004.

Touré. "The Hip-Hop Nation: Whose Is It? In the End, Black Men Must Lead." *The Hip-Hop Reader.* Eds. Tim Strode and Tim Wood. New York: Pearson Longman 2008.

Tyree, Tia C. M. "Lovin' Momma and Hatin' on Baby Mama: A Comparison of Misogynistic and Stereotypical Representations in Songs about Rappers' Mothers and Baby Mamas." *Women & Language* 32.2 (2009): 50-58.

West, Candace, and Don H. Zimmerman. "Doing Gender." *Gender and Society* 1.2 (1987): 125-51.

Wuthnow, Robert. "Democratic Renewal and Cultural Inertia: Why Our Best Efforts Fall." *Sociological Forum* 20.3 (2005): 343-67.

2.

"Mom Be Pimpin'"

Exploring the Mother-Whore Dichotomy in Hip-Hop

NICHOLAS POWERS

WHERE'S THE LOVE? It's the question that African-American pastors, progressive college students, cultural critics and "Old School" fans have been asking commercial Hip-Hop with increasing passion. The focal point of the debate is the imagery of African-American women as male rappers market themselves by displaying oiled video-vixens as advertisements of their virility. The contention being that the selling of the pole-dancing, breast-baring, booty-clapping, hyper-sexualized Black female body reinforces the racist imagery used to justify social policy that assaults the African-American family (Rose 181). And yet above the video-stew of body parts we see the shining face of the mother. Male paeans to maternal loyalty are a tradition within rap music ranging from 2Pac's 1995 "Dear Mama," Ghostface Killah's 1996 "All That I Got Is You" to Kanye West's 2005 "Hey Mama."

The binary between the sacred mother and the many fallen women suggests a Mother/Whore complex that has become deeply absorbed within Hip-Hop. My goals are to open a fissure in the dead-locked debate around rap music as a genre that either reflects reality or creates it and to explore how its Mother/Whore complex is based on a generation of African-American male hysteria.

Ultimately, my hope is to empower the voices of male feminists who write in and about Hip-Hop. Male feminists occupy a tense intellectual space of overlap as the beneficiaries of patriarchy and as witnesses to its interior dynamics. Our responsibility is to expose the blind privileges it creates and make an accounting of the social cost.

RAP AS MIRROR OR FACTORY

Hip-Hop has long been used as a moral trampoline. In his epic history *Can't Stop, Won't Stop*, Jeff Chang links Tipper Gore's parental advisory sticker crusade, Christian Fundamentalists trying to ban 2 Live Crew and former president Bill Clinton blasting Sistah Souljah during his first campaign into battle scenes of a Culture War that was a proxy for class war. Principled critiques have also been leveled at commercial Hip-Hop from within Black America. In 1993 Rev. Calvin Butts of the Abyssinian Baptist Church denounced from the pulpit "vulgar" rap music and after the sermon, dumped boxes of CDs in front of the Manhattan offices of Sony. In his 2004 video "Tip Drill," Cornel Hayes Jr., better known as the rapper Nelly, swiped a credit card between a woman's buttocks. Students of Spellman College, a historically Black female college, prepared to protest him at a charity event he was to host on campus. Nelly declined to show. In 2007 shock jock Don Imus called the women of the Rutgers University basketball team "nappy-headed hoes." He was fired but the controversy turned into a referendum on Hip-Hop. It peaked that year in two televised debates. The first one was Oprah's Town Hall and the next "Hip Hop vs. America" on Black Tree TV. Panelists from critic Stanley Crouch, rappers Nelly, Chuck D. and business mogul Russell Simmons debated the impact of rap music. No final answer was found but more importantly neither was the right question.

The debate around Hip-Hop is a vortex of loyalties. Progressives are wary of critiquing rap music, fearing it will reinforce the conservative alibi of "Black pathology" that is used to strip needed social programs. Yet rappers often dodge their responsibility by posing as urban witnesses, beleaguered entrepreneurs or innocent entertainers. The vacuum of accountability cedes conservatives the moral high ground that becomes a segregated place, accessible only upon acceptance of more conservatism (Rose 5-6). Hence the debate swings between two poles; either Hip-Hop is an innocent mirror of reality or manufactures a warped version of it. On the Oprah Town Hall, Simmons said, "The Hip-Hop community is a mirror, a reflection of the dirt we overlook—the violence, the misogyny, the sexism." On "Hip Hop vs. America" Crouch said, "If you make a sexist video, if you make a dehumanizing video, if you reduce a female to a bitch, a hoe, if you elevate a pimp; you have done something wrong." My first intervention is to collapse the either/or of the initial question to ask not if Hip-Hop mirrors or manufactures reality but how "mirroring" manufactures social reality.

Ideology is how strangers within closed borders know each other without ever meeting. Imagery is a vital part of ideology as it outlines roles for people to act or determines what we expect from others. Benedict Anderson showed in *Imagined Communities* how members "of even the smallest nation will never know most of their fellow-members, meet them, or even hear of them, yet in the minds of each lives the image of their communion" (2006: 6-7). Hip-Hop inherited and recreated the visual vocabulary of race that existed for centuries as a social scale of value by which European immigrants could navigate the "New World." In a painful irony, rappers have continued this iconography of white supremacist communion.

Before the United States existed images of "Blackness" circulated in the trade routes between the metropoles of Europe to the colonies that clutched the edge of an unknown continent. Europeans were told of the New World before migrating, saw imagery of "Negroe" slaves before meeting them (Jordan 23). The generative ideology of race created images of the enslaved that justified their role in the plantation economy and portrayed the Black female body as the site of lascivious animality that invited force (Jordan 79; Blassingame 154; Douglass 396). The caricatures of the Mammy, Coon, Brute and Jezebel swelled and ebbed throughout American history as each wave of Europeans contrasted their whiteness on this darkness. Even if they never met African-Americans, it was the "image of their communion," the currency on which was printed the wage of their whiteness (Roediger 12-13). Poorly paid European immigrants were compensated with "white" privileges, one part of which was the vocabulary of dehumanization for "negroes." Whites in the U.S. have historically had an appetite for racist caricatures and many African-Americans have a great fear and suspicion of those representations.

Within this overarching history, we can see Hip-Hop more clearly. By the 1970s the Bronx was gouged by the Cross-Bronx Expressway, working families were stacked into concrete towers and schools closed as arson fires gutted buildings. The ethnically diverse youth of the region grew up in the shadow of this ruin. Yet amidst the rubble they began to create a culture. Nelson George in *Hip Hop America* wrote of first hearing rap music in 1978, "I was ordering lunch when a teenager came strutting by ... he was jamming a tape with a man talking very fast in rhyme over,

I believe, 'Love Is the Message'" (23). It was a year before Sugar Hill Gang released "Rapper's Delight." DJ Kool Herc was just starting to blast people with his Herculoid speakers. Hip-Hop was small and local but slowly it seeped into the city, beyond the Nuyorican crews break-dancing in the park or kids ciphering on the corner; Hip-Hop injected itself into the distribution chains of an interconnected global capitalist economy. In the beginning, it had diverse rappers from party lover Heavy D to round the way girl MC Lyte to gangster rapper Ice-T. Although DJs and rappers were moving into wider distribution throughout the 1980s and racking impressive sales, it was not until 1991 when Soundscan was installed that the profit potential of Hip-Hop was revealed. By passing the CD over the laser reader, accurate sales records could be tallied that determined the position of music on the Billboard charts.[1]

Sales showed that white people were interested in rap music and the industry moved in to sell it. Over the 1990s Hip-Hop was extracted out of the communities that created it, where it had been one among a number of self-affirming discourses that defined "Blackness." Marketing rap to a mainstream white audience changed the production of it. In order to cater to the white imagination, pre-existing images such as the Coon, Jezebel and Brute were re-created in rap as the Pimp, Ho and Gangsta. Two generations after it began, the original aesthetic diversity of Hip-Hop has narrowed to gangsta clichés that wall African-American youth within an over-powering narrative of "Blackness" that is not a creative expression of life as it is an unsatisfactory commercial substitute. Commercial Hip-Hop has become a historical force, helping to sustain in its hyper-sexualized, materialistic and ultimately racist plantation imagery, the very material and ideological conditions that created it. Ideas and images that reinforce white supremacy are now the measuring stick of authentic Blackness.

The question of whether Hip-Hop mirrors or manufactures reality eludes the fact that social reality is an act of mirroring. Marxist philosopher Louis Althusser, in *Lenin and Philosophy,* defined ideology as the "imaginary relationship of individuals to their real conditions of existence" (162). My concern is that to the extent that Hip-Hop reinvents classic images of white supremacy, specifically transforming the Jezebel stereotype into a cornucopia of slander such as the video-vixen, ho, tip-drill and jump-off, it creates an imaginary world, which blinds listeners to the reality of their own existence.

Yet Althusser also asked, "Why do men 'need' this imaginary trans-position of their real conditions of existence in order to 'represent to themselves' their real conditions of existence?" (164) He answers this question by introducing the classic scene of being "hailed" in which an individual is transformed into a subject of ideology by recognizing the call (171-176). The scene works on the assumption of an empty individual who is constituted through material practice, but what if no individual is empty? What if that individual is filled with personal and generational dynamics that allow some acts of ideological hailing to take hold and not others? The question can be re-phrased. Why are male rappers so vulnerable to the white supremacist hailing of Black women as Jezebels? Why rhyme about the many women used and tossed away but hold above the fallen women the pure mother? We see this in a series of songs celebrating mothers from 2Pac's 1995 "Dear Mama," Beanie Sigel with *Scarface* in 2001 with "Mom Praying" to Kanye West's 2005 "Hey Mama."

The relevance of this question is not limited to a small set of rappers. It asks whether they articulate a psychological complex shared by a generation. Hip-Hop came into existence at a time of great transformation for African-American families. In 1965 Daniel Moynihan wrote *The Negro Family: The Case for National Action*, which argued that the cause "of the deterioration of the fabric of Negro society is the deterioration of the Negro family." The report sets the institution of slavery and the socio-economic oppression that followed as causal agents for absent fathers, matriarchal households and a "tangle of pathology." The report was critiqued for advocating patriarchy as a solution for racial oppression and for situating the pathology among African-Americans rather than in the institutions of white racism. His use of Black damage imagery, a tradition of motifs that show African-Americans as broken and requiring either assistance or social quarantine was, to be fair, used by Left activists and Afrocentrists. If too easily shifting the cause from institutional racism to the family, the Moynihan Report was prophetic in that it located where the effects of racial oppression would become increasingly more visible. Since 1960, the percentage of Black children living in single parent homes has doubled from 22 percent to 53 percent. Since 1980 most Black children have been raised by single-mothers. In 2007, the rate of single-parent households among African-Americans was 65 percent. It was into this era of plummeting social services, underemployment, mass incarceration, "benign neglect," crumbling cities and absent fathers that Hip-Hop was born. Decades later, young men who survived and became rappers, would praise the mothers who "held it down" while simultaneously using the very aforementioned damage imagery to degrade women.

THE MALE HYSTERIC

If Hip-Hop shows us a variation of the Mother/Whore complex let's turn to Sigmund Freud's 1912 essay *The Most Prevalent Form of Degradation in Erotic Life* in which it was first defined. The infant experiences caretaking as a sensual act and as it matures to puberty, erotic feeling flows into the grooves of touch left by the parent. Yet they are damned by the figure of the father, who bars the mother as an object through which this feeling can be satisfied. According to Freud the normal course of development is to find surrogates. What triggers the Mother/Whore complex is either the lack of those surrogates or the gravity of maternal memory. Whether from frustration or attraction, the erotic feeling turns and charges the original images and locks on them and the ego, and in order to protect itself buries that desire in the unconscious. As the subject's eroticism is fixated on barred fantasies the only way to free sensuality is to choose objects that do not evoke the maternal memory or to degrade the lover. Freud wrote, "Where such men love they have no desire and where they desire there cannot be love" (52).

In Freud's Oedipal scenario the father comes between the child and mother. In the generations since, modern psychoanalysts have translated the biological father as an abstract "paternal function" that is necessary to split the mother child symbiosis and launch the child into language (Mitchell and Rose; Dor 1998). In the Pre-Oedipal scene the boy asks "what does the mother want," locates the object of her desire, and tries to embody it. Later he renounces being this "phallus" in order to have it. Yet in rap songs of maternal praise this paternal function is corrupted and the phallus is missing. In "Dear Mama" 2Pac raps in his hurt husky voice "No love from my daddy 'cause the coward wasn't there. He passed away and I didn't cry, 'cause my anger wouldn't let me feel for a stranger." Tupac represents the classic lament of the hysteric who shares with the mother the hurt of being betrayed by the father and has the passionate need to replace him. His life is a quest to embody an illusionary ideal and therefore he suffers from performance anxiety, from the need to "show" that he has the "phallus" because his biological father did not. In his excellent book *The Clinical Lacan*, therapist Joel Dor writes on the hysterical male,

> The hysteric often experiences himself as not having been loved enough by the other, as not having received the full evidence of love he expected from his mother. This frustration in love always comes under the heading of what is at stake with regard to the phallus. Thus the hysteric sees himself as a pathetic object of his mother's desire, as opposed to what would be a complete and ideal object, the phallus. (1999: 80)

The physical father was absent and could not be the ideal "phallus," so the son tries to embody it for his mother who is suffering from its lack. We can see this psychological structure in the lyrics of Jay-Z. His song "Anything" from the 2000 debut album *The Truth* by Beanie Sigel, decries what his mother had to become to insure their survival. He raps:

> Thanks for holdin' down the household when times was bad, as the man, I apologize for my dad. When the rent was due, you would hustle like a pimp would do, that wasn't the life meant for you. You're a queen, you deserve the cream, everything that gleamed, everything that shines, everything that's mine.

Here he acknowledges the symbolic debt of labor owed to society by the father that the mother took on. Jay-Z's mom had to "hustle like a pimp" assuming a role that degraded her and separated her from her son even as it provided for them. Jay-Z wants to be what his mother lacked, to do work and play the role for his mother that his dad should have done. Are we listening to the lyrics of a hysteric?

In Lacanian psychoanalysis the phallus, which is the object of the mother's desire other than the child and is what separates them, is in the view of the hysteric male a degraded object not worthy of intruding upon the mother/child bond. The hysteric does not surrender to castration but instead ceaselessly tries to prove to the mother that he does have the phallus, and that he can be everything she needs. We see this in Jay-Z's lyrics in that the father that separates them is a degraded man, an absent man, who mother had to become in working like a "pimp."

The wealth that Jay-Z secures is how he defines his desirability, how he proves he was the "phallus" that his father was not. In turn, he will amass huge amounts of it, beyond the satisfaction of any immediate need because it is meant to be poured into the ephemeral hands of his mother's memory. And it will never be enough. The dollars, the credit cards, the houses and stocks fall through those hands because in the end, they are not real but the memory of hunger and hopelessness around which he created the character of Jay-Z.

The "pimp" she had to be is a role her son Jay-Z now labors to fulfill but which is still a performance that must go on in perpetuity since as Dor writes, "the hysteric's chief desire is that his desire remain unsatisfied." Jay-Z must be continually dissatisfied with women so that he can continue to be satisfied with himself. So he can produce himself as that which his mother lacked—the money that the absent father did not provide and the money she was forced to leave him to make.

If we extrapolate from Jay-Z and view his life in the context of a larger social pattern then the possibility exists that a generational male hysteria complex is feeding into the white supremacist vision of the Jezebel. We are witnessing a male subjectivity that in the end necessitates the equation of the one maternal exception surrounded by the many degraded women. If a woman ever saw behind the mask of the pimp she would see the boy who needs to be seen as man because he has not yet become one. If one contrasts Jay-Z's "Anything" with his "Big Pimpin'" we can see an extreme Mother/Whore dichotomy emerge:

I'm a pimp in every sense of the word bitch, better trust than believe them,
in the cut where I keep 'em, til I need a nut, til I need to beat the guts, then its, beep-beep and I'm pickin' em up, let em play with the dick in the truck.
Many chicks wanna put Jigga fists in cuffs, divorce him and split his bucks.
Just because you got good head, I'ma break bread, so you can live it up?
Shit I parts with nothin', y'all be frontin, me give my heart to a woman?
Not for nothing, never happen.

The first sentence is a first-person testament to a woman listener of his power, emotional distance and control over women's roles in his life. He then raps in third person, returning to first person to ask rhetorical questions about her worth to him, accusing the anonymous woman of parasitical behavior and assuring himself and us that he will never be split from his wealth by her.

The position of utterance from first or third person is a measurement of the distance between the speaker and the language, between staging a pose or embodying the words. Second is the arc of self-making against the threat posed by a woman who could dissolve him and split him apart from the wealth and power that constitute his subjectivity. It hinges on the use of the word "pimp" since he claims it as title, a quilting point to his self. Jay-Z must degrade women and present them as parasitical beings who want to consume his performance. Again, Dor provides us with a useful quote:

> The hysteric's phallic narcissism most often takes the spectacular and unmodulated form of 'putting on a show', that is of staging a performance in which his primary goal is to offer himself as the embodiment of the ideal object of desire. The hysteric must therefore identify with this object bodily as well as through speech. The essential thing is to appear as a brilliant object that will fascinate the other. (1999: 81)

Returning to Jay-Z's first lyrics in "Big Pimpin'," we can see him perform the persona of the pimp or as Dor would say, "putting on a show" that defines him as an object of desire. In the gaze of the imagined predatory woman, he is a walking ATM. She reaffirms his wealth and sexual virility. She also must never be a "pure" woman or a mother surrogate because it will mean Jay-Z would have to become emotionally transparent and lead to an exposure of the anxiety of not being enough. So he must create images of degraded women in order to maintain desire. The hysteric is constantly putting on a show to prove he has the phallus, that he is the 'pimp' that dad should have been, in the sense of earning money for the household, he is driven to endlessly acquire evidence for a insecurity he cannot admit he has.

When we return to Jay-Z's "Big Pimpin'", "Many chicks wanna put Jigga fists in cuffs, divorce him and split his bucks, just because you got good head, I'ma break bread, so you can live it up? shit I parts with nothin', y'all be frontin'," we can read here a fear of women. They threaten him with dissolution, by enticing him with sex and intimacy, by 'frontin' as an honest lover they could become like his mother, a maternal-surrogate who he would then owe everything. He fears having his wealth split by a fake mother-surrogate, an imposter who could not offer the total love that he expects. If being a pimp, a wealthy and virile and emotionally distant man, is how he secures the wealth that his mother never had then he needs ho's, skanks, hood-rats and bitches around him to be the evidence of his authenticity. Degraded Black women are a psychological necessity for the Black male hysteric rapper.

So again, why does Jay-Z, like other male rappers, degrade women into tip-drills, ho's, hood-rats and bitches? As Dor writes,

> Such a subject ... in order to maintain his desire, tries never to supply a possible fulfilling object for that desire ... the resulting dissatisfaction remobilizes his desire in an aspiration, always more and more remote, toward an ideal of being. (1999: 80)

The remote ideal mother, a shining exception, whose gaze he both tries to keep focused on him and is locked in, must never see that it is a show, a performance. Other women must be kept at a safe distance, so that they never have a chance at becoming the mother-surrogate and hence see that "everything that shines, everything that's mine" is really an emptiness that dissolves upon contact.

The fallen father, the lost phallus and the attempt to perform it are a Hip-Hop tropes. In his autobiographical movie, 50 Cent plays himself, showing us the arc of his self-becoming. We see him as a young boy, lost in the streets after his mother was killed by a rival drug dealer. The one direction that stands clear is living her unlived life, dealing and also being shot and surviving it to emerge on the other side a man. At the end of the movie, 50 leans into a mirror, "All these years I was looking for my father but I was just looking for myself."

[1]"Soundscan's innovation was to install a bar-code reading point-of-purchase system to tally actual sales.... Independently distributed N.W.A.'s Efil4zaggin debuted at number two. At the same time dozens of big-bank pop and rock acts tumbled off the charts" (Chang 416).

WORKS CITED

Althusser, Louis. *Lenin and Philosophy*. Trans. Benn Brewster. New York: Monthly Review Press, 1971.

Anderson, Benedict. *Imagined Communities*. New York: Verso, 2006.

Black Tree TV. "Hip Hop vs. America." Web. <http://my.blacktree.tv/video/video/search?q=hip+vs+america>.

Blassingame, John W. *The Slave Community: Plantation Life in the Antebellum South*. New York: Oxford University Press, 1979.

Chang, Jeff. *Can't Stop, Won't Stop: A History of the Hip-Hop Generation*. New York: Picador, 2005.

Dor, Joel. *Introduction to the Reading of Lacan*. New York: Other Press, 1998.

Dor, Joel. *The Clinical Lacan*. New York: Other Press, 1999.

Douglass, Frederick. "Narrative of the Life of Frederick Douglass." *Norton Anthology of African American Literature*. New York: W. W. Norton & Company, 2005.

George, Nelson. *Hip Hop America*. New York: Penguin Books, 1998.

Jordan, Winthrop. *The White Man's Burden: Historical Origins of Racism in the United States*. New York: Oxford University Press, 1974.

Levy, Clifford. "Harlem Protest of Rap Lyrics Draws Debate and Steamroller." *The New York Times* 6 June 1993, New York Edition: C6-7.

Mitchell, Juliet and Jacqueline Rose, eds. *Feminine Sexuality: Jacques Lacan and the ecole freudienne*. New York: Pantheon Books, 1985.

Moynihan, Daniel Patrick. *The Negro Family: The Case for National Action*. Washington, DC: Office of Policy Planning and Research, U.S. Department of Labor, 1965.

Roediger, David. *The Wages of Whiteness: Race and the Making of the American Working Class*. New York: Verso, 1991.

Rose, Tricia. *The Hip Hop Wars: What We Talk About When We Talk About Hip Hop and Why It Matters*. New York: Basic Books, 2008.

Willens, Kathy. "Black College Women Take Aim at Rappers." Associated Press. 23 Apr. 2004. Web. <http://www.usatoday.com/life/music/news/2004-04-23-spelman-protest-rappers_x.htm>.

Winfrey, Oprah. "A Hip Hop Town Hall." April 2007. Web. <http://www.oprah.com/slideshow/oprahshow/oprahshow1_ss_20070417>.

3.
Making Room for
"Dear Mama" in Rap Music

ERIK NIELSON

IN 1992, WHEN SNOOP DOGG DECLARED that "Bitches ain't nothin' but ho's and tricks," he was not only delivering his own indictment of women, but he was also laying out the prescription for commercial success in the rap industry over the ensuing decades. Although there have been some notable exceptions, over the last 20 years, rap has become increasingly defined by what T. Denean Sharpley-Whiting calls a "'pimp-playa-bitch-ho' nexus" (xvii) and as a result, fans of mainstream rap music find it more and more difficult to escape the hyper-masculine, woman-bashing rhetoric that saturates the airwaves or the images of sexual objectification that have become commonplace in music videos. While in recent years this has led to a backlash of sorts among rap fans and scholars alike, who have criticized the gender politics that have emerged in rap, even a casual perusal of best-selling tracks—with titles like "Smack That" and "Lollipop"—suggests that rap artists have yet to respond in any meaningful way. What we are frequently left with instead is the sense that for rappers, women have little to offer as peers, partners, or role models. As Joan Morgan puts it, "half of them act like it wasn't a woman who clothed and fed their black asses" (69).

That's not entirely true. In fact, amidst all of the tracks that foreground men as playas or pimps and women as their tricks, bitches, or ho's, there is a small subgenre of songs in which rappers pay tribute to their single mothers, and what we find within these "mother tracks" is a stark contrast to the pimp/trick model that prevails elsewhere in rap. Within these songs, mothers are generally presented as strong and dependable authority figures, often by the same rappers (including Snoop Dogg himself) who gleefully denigrate women, revel in their weakness, and present them as mere objects of sexual desire in much of their work. Speaking to this exception for mothers that rappers have carved out, Natalie Hopkinson and Natalie Moore write, "In the commercial hip-hop lyrics themselves, women enjoy a largely schizophrenic existence.... Either 'My Mama is the best in whole wide world' or 'Bitch, eat my balls'" (86).[1] As Hopkinson and Moore rightly suggest with the term "schizophrenic," it is difficult to reconcile the exalted status of mothers with the degradation of womanhood that we find throughout rap, yet it is at the site of these contradictory impulses that I would like to situate this essay, paying particular attention to what mother tracks can reveal about the potential for female empowerment within rap as a genre.

As I hope to show by surveying a wide range of mother tracks, the mother figure occupies a unique space within rap's discourse. Although femininity is generally represented as antithetical to rap's ever-important masculine ethos, in mother tracks we find a recognition that the masculine power projected by so many rappers is often dependent on female strength. It becomes clear that as the sole caregivers within their families, the single mothers portrayed in these songs not only assume an authority and power generally associated with men, but function as the primary role models after which rappers pattern themselves, permitting them a level of reverence that is withheld from most other women. Put another way, the mother figure challenges the traditional gender roles found in rap, and in doing so she creates a rare space for male rappers to acknowledge the significant contributions of women in their own lives and, by extension, to rap overall.

"MOMMA LOVED ME, POP LEFT ME"[2]

In most mother tracks there are no fathers. In some songs, fathers' absence from their families is reinforced by their complete absence from the lyrics, but in several others, rappers go out of their way to emphasize the sense of abandonment that they feel as a result of having fathers who walked out on them. For example, in "Dear Mama,"[3] after describing the hardships faced by his "poor, single mother on welfare," 2Pac goes on to address his anger at the man who left his family in such dire straits:

Now ain't nobody tell us it was fair.
No love from my daddy cause the coward wasn't there.

He passed away and I didn't cry, cause my anger
wouldn't let me feel for a stranger.
They say I'm wrong and I'm heartless, but all along
I was lookin' for a father he was gone.

Ghostface Killah offers a similar perspective in "All I Got is You" when he says, "Sadly, daddy left me at the age of six," at first internalizing the loss of his father ("daddy left *me*") and then considering the impact on the rest of the family, beginning with his mother. He says, "I guess mommy wasn't strong enough—she just went down," and with her went the rest of the family, forced to share a cramped, roach-infested apartment with several other family members, often so poor that they had to beg the neighbors for food. Here and elsewhere, it becomes clear that the struggles many mothers were forced to endure came because of failed fathers—the male role models who weren't. Hence, in mother tracks specifically, gender roles are reversed, with male weakness figured as the obstacle that female strength must overcome.

To provide the support that their children need, these mothers—who are, as Lord Jamar (a member of Brand Nubian) reminds us, "young and so tender" themselves ("Momma")—often turn to their own mothers, calling on them to step in for absent fathers and raise two generations of children. To reinforce the grandmother's role as a stand-in for the fathers who have walked out, rappers often juxtapose their appearance with the disappearance of the fathers they are essentially replacing. Jay Z raps, "Momma loved me, pop left me. / Grandma dressed me, plus she fed me" ("Blueprint (Momma Loves Me)"). Similarly, Ghostface Killah places his mother's despair when his father left alongside the first introduction of his grandmother in the song, saying, "She cried, and grandma held the family down." The presence of grandmothers within these tracks is not surprising. For one, they have long been particularly important to African American families, serving as what E. Franklin Frazier called the "guardians of the generations." But over the last four decades, as fatherlessness has risen, especially in the African American community, so too has the need for grandmothers to step in and become the caregivers for their grandchildren (Ruiz 64). Like their daughters, these grandmothers are also generally single, and so what we find in these mother tracks, where grand*fathers* are conspicuously absent too, is a mirror of the broader trend of intergenerational fatherlessness, which places an increasing burden on mothers' mothers to raise their children's children.

With fatherlessness such an important factor in determining social outcomes and putting such a strain on mothers, we might expect that in these mother tracks rappers would be highly critical of the fathers who left their families in such desperate conditions. However, they are oddly silent on the issue. In calling his father a "coward," 2Pac goes farther than most others, some of whom express a surprising affection for the men who showed them so little. In "Blueprint (Momma Loves Me)," for instance, Jay Z repeats the line "Momma loved me, pop left me," but rather than emphasize the consequences of his father's decisions, he focuses instead on forgiveness, saying, "Momma raised me, pop I miss you./ God help me forgive him, I got some issues." In songs that are often about the hardship and suffering of whole families left by fathers, rappers' apparent unwillingness to tackle these men head-on is telling. For one, it suggests a tacit acceptance of a failed model of fatherhood, one in which absenteeism is the norm. We can see this in a rare father track called "Poppa was a Playa," in which Nas chronicles the drug use and infidelities of his father, yet he is far from critical of the man who leaves his hard-working mother—who "sacrifices all she got to feed us"—to cry by the phone when her husband doesn't come home. Nas's father, a jazz musician (hence the double meaning of "playa"), has little regard for the need to be a role model, but because he is physically present most of the time, he gets something of a pass. At one point, Nas confronts him for his cheating and drug use, only to be manipulated into lying to his mother:

> So then I asked him,
> "What's this white shit on that plate and your face, and
> Papa why you butt ass from the waist,
> and who's this lady I'm facing?"
> Dark skin you're not my mommy—
> he grabbed me up to run some smooth words by me,
> promised me things that he would buy me
> if I kept my mouth closed and don't tell mommy.

While we might be tempted to condemn his father's behavior and expect Nas to do the same, he explains that he can't because even though his father makes for a questionable role model, at least he was around when most other dads weren't: "So many kids I knew, never knew what pop was. / That's why I show my pop love." By the end of the track, we are left with a bleak assessment of fatherhood, which has become so degraded that finding men who take even a limited interest in their children becomes a cause for celebration—or at least a song in their honor.[4]

That Nas's father is a musician who openly womanizes and uses drugs reminds us of the lifestyle that many rappers endorse for themselves, and it suggests another reason why, as a result, they may be unwilling to attack their fathers. That is, rappers often find themselves on shaky ground from which to pass judgment, and by criticizing their fathers they would shine a spotlight on their own behavior. When men like 2Pac, Snoop Dogg, Kanye West, or Jay Z rap about how many women they've slept with in their other songs, with little attention to the consequences of their behavior, we are left to wonder how many struggling mothers are left in their wake. Put another way, how could Jay Z attack his father for lacking devotion to his family when elsewhere he drops pearls of wisdom like "I hit you with this advice: / Life's short, so play hard and stick hard /and the only time you love 'em is when your dick hard"? ("Cashmere Thoughts"). Thus, while rappers clearly convey their genuine appreciation for their mothers and the sacrifices they have made, they often stop short of any broader critique, perhaps because of their own role in perpetuating the social ills they had to endure themselves.

"FOR SO LONG SHE HAD TO BE STRONG"[5]

Rappers are, however, quite candid about perpetuating social problems as children, often describing their bad (and sometimes illegal) behavior, but also the severe punishments they could expect from their mothers if they got caught. One of the most intriguing similarities to emerge from these songs is that they often pause to describe, in reverential tone, the beatings that mothers regularly doled out.[6] For example, in "Momma Can You Hear Me?" Talib Kweli tells us that his mother "roasted my ass when I was bad" and that he could expect "beatin's" any time he was caught lying.[7] Talking back to these mothers apparently wasn't a good idea either—in "Guess Who," Gipp tells us that "Talkin' back only got you closer to Southern Bell" which "got your forehead swell" and earlier in the song, Khujo describes a similar consequence for disobedience, saying, "Guess who beat the dog shit outta me, kid? / My momma didn't play, shit, I had to pick the switches." Even grandmothers are described as being fearsome—Beanie Sigel opens "Mom Praying" with "Eight decades and four years and gran still kickin'. / Look at ma, still whippin'. / Still keep a strap, won't hesitate to give the kids whippins." In these mother tracks and others, it is clearly important to establish the mother's physical dominance over her household, at least in part because it allows the rappers to show the kind of respect that is normally reserved for men. In describing the beatings he took, Talib Kweli says to his mother, "[You] played the role of dad when you had to," reminding us that, especially in the universe of rap music, the kind of power wielded by these mothers, and the respect it demands, is almost always associated with masculinity.[8]

The depictions of physical punishments appear to be part of a broader strategy of masculinizing—or at least desexualizing—the mothers in these songs. It's worth noting that male presence has been largely cleared away, with almost no mention of men in the lives of either the rappers or their mothers. In one rare instance, Kanye West mentions a man in his mother's life, but as with the other men in these mothers' lives, he brings nothing but grief. Recalling a childhood memory, West offers a moving scene in which he had to provide comfort to his mother, an inversion of the typical order in mother tracks. He says,

> Seven years old, caught you with tears in your eyes
> 'cause a nigga cheat and telling you lies, then I started to cry.
> (Hey Mama)
> As we knelt on the kitchen floor
> I said mommy I'm a love you 'til you don't hurt no more.

With male presence once again equated to female victimization, it becomes clear why West's inclusion of another man is an anomaly in songs usually concerned with establishing mothers as unflappable pillars of support. What's far more common is a concerted effort to imbue mothers with masculine strength, either by explicitly equating them to fathers, or by attributing to them characteristics reserved for men. Jay Z, for instance, in describing his mother's attempts to raise rent money, refers to her as a *pimp*: "When the rent was due, you would hustle like a pimp would do" ("Anything"). The use of the word "pimp" to describe a woman scraping together enough money to pay the rent is an obvious misappropriation of the term, especially as it's used in rap, where pimps are prized as men who are rolling in cash that is gained from "the commodification of sex and the private ownership of women's bodies" (Kelley 1997: 72).[9] Jay Z's incongruous use of "pimp" to describe his mother represents his refusal to portray her in the victimized role Kanye West does, preferring instead to associate her, however problematically, with the figure of black male authority that he and many other rappers so openly embrace in other songs.[10]

What makes these mothers worthy of tribute is that they are strong enough to take on the roles of father and mother at once, and so for all the masculinization that we find within these songs, we also find depictions of the mothers in their more traditional roles as nurturers. Both Talib Kweli and Ghostface Killah, for example, offer almost identical images of a mother standing over her son each morning, wiping the "cold" from his eyes before letting him leave the house, while in other tracks, rappers talk about their sickness as children and their mothers' ability to comfort them.[11] 2Pac, for instance, says to his mother, "When I was sick as a little kid / to keep me happy there's no limit to the things you did," and Gipp reminds each of his listeners that it was "Momma" who was "the first to change your diaper when your stomach wasn't calm." Jay Z offers similar words of appreciation, too, when he says, "Thanks for the days you kept me breathing when my asthma was bad / and my chest was weezin'. Thanks for the look of love" ("Anything"). In all of these examples, the physical vulnerabilities experienced by the rappers as children serve as fitting representations of the much broader set of challenges faced—and overcome—with the nurturing help of their mothers.

Nowhere is their ability to overcome these challenges more apparent than in the nearly universal emphasis on food found throughout these mother tracks. In some, the mother's ability to procure food is represented, in and of itself, as a significant achievement in such impoverished circumstances. 2Pac tells us that his "Mama made miracles every Thanksgiving," while she was "just workin' with the scraps [she] was given," reminding us that in these homes just providing the basic necessities of life stretched their mothers thin. (In "All That I Got is You," Ghostface Killah makes such realities clear when he describes his family's reliance on the free lunch "that held us down like steel" or the embarrassing moments when he had to ask the neighbors for extra food.) In other tracks, however, the rappers pause over the food itself, as Beanie Sigel does when he describes "My favorite, a pot of rice and her stewed chicken" or Kanye West, describing his mother's chicken soup as the cure for a winter cold: "You fix me up something that was good for my soul, / Famous home chicken soup—can I have another bowl?" West's description of his mother's food as being good for his "soul"—echoed by Talib Kweli who says that his mother would "feed my soul with home cookin'"—indicates the extent to which the food that simmers throughout these songs transcends its literal significance, functioning as a symbol not only of corporeal nourishment, but also of the spiritual strength that these mothers have managed to impart to their sons.

The use of the word "soul" also hints at these mothers' roles in shaping their sons as *musicians*, and in a couple of instances, rappers actually expand on this distinctly musical influence. Jay Z remembers the weekends when his mother would have music playing, telling her, "I was ok with not having everything / long as Saturdays you had the Commodores playing." Here music is formulated as a stand-in for the things the family lacked, a kind of "soul food" that, at least for Jay Z, was the ticket to putting actual food (and a great deal more) on his table later in life. And Snoop Dogg insists that his mother "taught me everything," including, it seems, his love for music, as one of the few specific memories he offers is of "bangin' oldies in the living room" with "the queen" in his life. What both of these tracks suggest is not just the importance of mothers generally, but "the striking ways in which (often young) mothers mediated the pop-cultural experiences of their sons" (Quinn 157). Especially among rappers like Jay Z and Snoop, who have long privileged masculinity in their music, mother tracks allow a unique way for them to keep it real by acknowledging the strong female figure who helped them become the men—and the rappers—they are now.[12]

And as grown men, they want to give something back. As we might predict, one thing that several mother tracks have in common is that rappers talk about their abilities to compensate for the years of financial hardship by lavishing gifts on their mothers. In "I Made It" Jay Z promises his mother that he's going to "make sure every day is Christmas," something that Kanye West seems intent on doing as well when he tells his mother, "I'm a get you a Jag, whateva else you want. / Just tell me what kind of S-Type Donda West like." Here and in other mother tracks, the rappers juxtapose their dependence and, at times, frailty as children with their newfound willingness to step in as caregivers, essentially reversing the roles of parent and child. Hence, alongside references to their mothers as "queens" or other authority figures, the rappers also frequently refer to them as "girls," as in the chorus to Brand Nubian's "Momma," which begins "I always loved my momma (She's my favorite girl)." While we might be tempted to read this as the typical posture among male rappers trying assert their own authority over everyone else's (particularly a woman's) what we find instead (or in addition) is the sense that the rappers are trying to step in, and fill the voids in their mothers' lives, in the process helping to rebuild the families that were barely held together by struggling women.[13] Having seen his mother and grandmother take generations of responsibilities onto their shoulders, Jay Z, like the other rappers, makes it clear that he's ready to do the same when he says, "Your baby boy's a made man. I'm a hold the fam' down like three generations" ("I Made It"). In contrasting "baby boy" with "made man," Jay Z reminds his mother—and us—of the immense distance he's travelled from boyhood to manhood, a journey he says he never would've completed without "the most beautiful girl in the world."

CONCLUSION

In 1987, Rakim famously declared "It ain't where you're from—it's where you're at" (Eric B and Rakim). But as these mother tracks can attest, rappers place great value on the role of the past—where they're from—in determining where they're at. In fact, one of the primary ways that rappers attempt to establish their authenticity, that they're "keeping it real," is by emphasizing their local affiliations and their connections to the people and places from their childhood. To quote Mobb Deep, in rap today "Fuck where you at, kid / it's where you're from," so perhaps it should come as no surprise that it is through depictions of the mother, the most literal representation of where rappers are *from*, that we find some of rap's clearest articulations of what it means to be authentic. Indeed, the very same qualities that we have seen make the mothers in these tracks exemplary—strength, resilience, and (most important of all) loyalty to family—are those that rappers project for themselves as well.

With fathers almost always out of the picture, it is the mother figure who becomes the model after which rappers pattern themselves, and so her unique embodiment of where they're from gives her a privileged position within a music that otherwise tends to exclude femininity from its identity formations.[14] As Poppa Wu tells us at the end of Ghostface Killah's "All I Got is You," for rappers, remembering their mothers is a necessary part of establishing themselves: "if you forget where you come from, you're never gonna make it where you're goin' because you lost the reality of yourself."

If, as these rappers tell us, that reality begins and ends with mothers, then within these songs we find an important representation of feminine presence underpinning masculine power, a tacit recognition that women are in many respects responsible for the growth and development of rappers—and therefore rap music. In that sense, mother tracks offer a conspicuous challenge to the misogyny that has come to dominate rap's themes and lyrics. And yet, tempted as we might be to embrace these poignant tributes to mothers as an antidote to that misogyny, we must also keep in mind that these songs eulogize mothers, not *motherhood*.[15] That is, while rappers are clearly willing to recognize the important contributions of their own mothers, that recognition doesn't translate into a broader consideration of the struggles facing Black women generally or mothers specifically.[16] Instead, the mothers in these songs occupy a privileged but segregated space, seemingly unable to wield their influence beyond the confines of individual songs and into the broader discourse of rap music. Until that changes, the extraordinary women presented in mother tracks will, unfortunately, remain postscripts in a genre that would do well to remember "Dear Mama" a little more often.

[1]Michael Eric Dyson also recognizes this "paradoxical but predictable trend" among rappers: "loving *my* mama while loathing my *baby's* mama" (23) (emphasis in original).

[2]From Jay-Z's "Blueprint (Momma Loves Me)."

[3]A note on orthography: in some songs, the preferred spelling is "momma," while in others it's "mama." In transcribing lyrics, I have tried to maintain rappers' preferences when they are clear. For example, if the title of a song includes the spelling "momma," that's also the spelling I use in my transcription of that song. The same goes for songs that

use "mama." In cases where there's no obvious preference, I have used "momma" as the default simply because that appears to be the more common spelling.

4Nas doesn't glorify his father at the expense of his mother, however. Not only does he acknowledge her contributions in this song, but after her death, he wrote his own mother track, "Dance," in which he says to her, "You was my strength to carry on and now I'm good."

5From Goodie Mob's "Guess Who."

6Violence in rap music is usually associated with masculinity, but as some of these tracks suggest in their depictions of extreme corporal punishment, some of this male violence may be learned at an early age by boys who go on to model the behavior of their mothers as well.

7"Momma Can You Hear Me" was not released on any of Kweli's albums but is nevertheless readily available online.

8In most tracks the mother's willingness to use physical punishment is viewed reverentially because it is associated with her power, but in "Momma" Grand Puba suggests that the beatings actually reveal the mother's victimization and subsequent projection onto her son. He says, "I remember as a kid, sometimes I used to think / you used to beat me for some shit that my daddy did." He quickly goes on to qualify the statement, saying "I realize, now I'm older and wise / when you used to put it on me still had love in your eyes," but it nevertheless raises the possibility that some of these physical punishments indicate a kind of *weakness* in the mother, as she takes out on her son (in many respects a proxy for the missing father) what she was unable to on his father.

9For decades, the pimp has been "an emblematic figure ... elevated to the status of hero" (Kelley 1996: 141) who, despite being a criminal, has been "a figure of fascination, a certain awe, and suppressed respect" because he has "always been viewed as a rare example of black male authority over his domain" (George 36-37). There are obvious problems, though, when this heroic figure is projected onto women, especially those who may have been mistreated by men in the past.

10This also sheds an important light on the "survival of the fittest" worldview within much of rap music, one in which the only way to avoid being a victim is to victimize. In trying to extol his mother's virtues, Jay Z places her in the morally questionable position of the pimp, associating her with a figure that is responsible for keeping women in a weakened and dependent state. This mother-as-pimp formulation raises questions similar to those about the hypocrisy of a rapper praising his mother in one song while denigrating women in many others.

[11]Ghostface Killah says, "But I remember this: moms would lick her finger tips / to wipe the cold out my eye before school wit her spit," compared to Talib Kweli's "Early morning, lick your fingers, wipe the cold from my eye."

[12]See Eithne Quinn (156-160) for a discussion of the way many gangsta rappers, including Ice Cube, Dr. Dre, and Snoop Dogg, represented themselves to the press, often by placing an emphasis on family (especially their mothers) not often found in their songs. As Quinn's discussion makes clear, their music was but one way they shaped their public identity, and if we look more closely at their extra-musical attempts at self-representation, we see more than the "flagrant and oft-noted nihilism in gangsta" (Quinn 157). Hence, the tributes we find in mother tracks are actually part of an even broader attempt within rap to acknowledge female strength, perhaps as an attempt to counter-balance the lyrics that more frequently undermine it.

[13]In "It's a Family Affair," Paul Gilroy objects to the use of family metaphors to describe black cultural politics because such metaphors often tend to minimize female roles. According to Gilroy, the discourse of race-as-family "attempts to interpret the crisis of black politics and social life as a crisis solely of black masculinity," a crisis that can be fixed by "instituting appropriate forms of masculinity and male authority" (92). When Jay Z declares that he will "hold the fam' down like three generations," he is, to some extent, illustrating the patriarchal logic that Gilroy takes issue with: as the "made man," he will step in and solve all of the problems the family has faced. At the same time, however, he and other rappers also make it clear that the family was, in fact, held down (however tenuously) by strong women. At least in this context, his desire to step in and become the caregiver is, I think, more productively interpreted as a desire to supply the missing male role model, but not necessarily one that will minimize or usurp the matriarchal authority that he has taken pains to depict. He is trying to step into a nurturing role and in doing so actually challenges typical definitions of masculinity that view "nurture and care and feminine and unmanly" (Dowd 181).

[14]That is not to ignore the important female rappers, such as Queen Latifah and Salt-N-Pepa, who have brought to the fore issues of gender in rap music, but to point out that their voices have been largely drowned

out by male rappers who have consistently undermined female presence in their work. For more on the ways in which these rappers (and others) have engaged feminist politics in their work, see Gwendolyn Pough's *Check it While I Wreck It.*

[15]Indeed, as Tia C. M. Tyree notes, the language rappers use to refer to the mother of their children (their baby mama) is often at complete odds with that used to refer to their own mothers. Whereas mothers are deserving of praise and adoration, baby mamas are often described as "worthless, unethical disrespectful gold diggers and freaks" (54). And Travis Gosa (in this volume), observing the disturbing dissonance between rappers' praise of their mothers and their utter disregard for other women, puts it this way: "Rappers present tearful prose to their mothers in one verse, while threatening to rape and kill everyone else's mother on the next track."

[16]In fact, when he describes his mother as "that one lady that no other woman could be, no matter what," Saigon expresses a sentiment found throughout these mother tracks. While this type of exclusivity is clearly intended to express an appreciation for the exceptional contributions of each mother, it also has the effect of limiting the songs' applicability to a wider group of women.

WORKS CITED

2Pac. "Dear Mama." *Me Against the World.* Jive, 1995.

Beanie Sigel. "Mom Praying." *The Reason.* Roc-a-Fella, 2001.

Brand Nubian. "Momma." *Fire in the Hole.* Babygrande Records, 2004.

Dowd, Nancy E. *Redefining Fatherhood.* New York: New York Press, 2000.

Dyson, Michael Eric. *Holler if You Hear Me: Searching for Tupac Shakur.* New York: Basic Civitas, 2001.

Eric B and Rakim. "In the Ghetto." *Let the Rhythm Hit 'Em.* MCA, 1990.

Frazier, E. Franklin. *Negro Family in the United States.* Chicago: University of Chicago Press, 1939.

George, Nelson. *Hip Hop America.* New York: Penguin, 1998.

Ghostface Killah. "All That I Got is You." *Ironman.* Razor Sharp/Epic Street, 1996.

Gilroy, Paul. "It's a Family Affair." In *That's the Joint! The Hip Hop Studies Reader.* Eds. Murray Forman and Mark Anthony Neal. New

York: Routledge, 2004. 87-94.

Goodie Mob. "Guess Who." *Soul Food*. La Face, 1995.

Hopkinson, Natalie and Natalie Y. Moore. *Deconstructing Tyrone: A New Look at Black Masculinity in the Hip-Hop Generation*. San Francisco: Cleis Press, 2006.

Jay Z. "Anything." On Beanie Sigel's *The Truth*. Roc-a-Fella, 2000.

Jay Z. "Blueprint (Momma Loves Me)." Roc-a-Fella, 2001.

Jay Z. "Cashmere Thoughts." *Reasonable Doubt*. EMI, 1996.

Jay Z. "I Made It." *Kingdom Come*. Roc-a-Fella, 2006.

Kanye West. "Hey Mama." *Late Registration*. Roc-a-Fella, 2005.

Kelley, Robin D. G. "Kickin' Reality, Kickin' Ballistics: Gangsta Rap and Postindustrial Los Angeles." *Droppin' Science: Critical Essays on Rap Music and Hip Hop Culture*. Ed. William Eric Perkins. Philadelphia: Temple University Press, 1996. 117-158.

Kelley, Robin D. G. *Yo' Mama's Dysfunktional: Fighting the Culture Wars in Urban America*. Boston: Beacon Press, 1997.

Mobb Deep. "Right Back at You." *The Infamous*. RCA, 1995.

Morgan, Joan. *When the Chickenheads Come Home to Roost*. New York: Simon and Schuster, 1999.

Nas. "Dance." *God's Son*. Sony, 2002.

Nas. "Poppa was a Playa." *The Lost Tapes*. Sony, 2002.

Pough, Gwendolyn. *Check it While I Wreck It: Black Womanhood, Hip-Hop Culture, and the Public Sphere*. Boston: Northeastern University Press, 2004.

Quinn, Eithne. *Nuthin' But a "G" Thang: The Culture and Commerce of Gangsta Rap*. New York: Columbia University Press, 2005.

Ruiz, Dorothy S. "The Changing Roles of African American Grandmothers Raising Grandchildren: An Exploratory Study in the Piedmont Region of North Carolina." *Western Journal of Black Studies* 32.1 (2008): 62-71.

Saigon. "If ... (My Mommy)." *Warning Shots*. Sure Shot Recordings, 2004.

Sharpley-Whiting, T. Denean. *Pimps Up, Ho's Down: Hip Hop's Hold on Young Black Women*. New York: New York University Press, 2007.

Snoop Dogg. "Bitches Ain't Shit" by Dr. Dre. *Chronic*. Death Row, 1992.

Snoop Dogg. "I Love my Momma." *No Limit Top Dogg*. Priority, 1999.

Talib Kweli. "Momma Can You Hear Me?" Unreleased. Available at <http://www.youtube.com>.

Tyree, Tia C. M. "Lovin' Momma and Hatin' on Baby Mama: A Comparison of Misogynistic and Stereotypical Representations in Songs about Rappers' Mothers and Baby Mamas." *Women & Language* 32.2 (2009): 50-58.

4.
Shine

A Queer Cosmology of Mothering from Audre Lorde to MeShell Ndegeocello

ALEXIS PAULINE GUMBS

Loving you was always a risk,
a shift to the meaning of the everyday.
Like spray paint to mural, cardboard to head spin,
disco break beat to party poem in the park,
you were not meant to be loved like this.
They say you were made to be used up by capital
and then thrown away when the jobs got outsourced.
Loving you is a creative act.

THIS CHAPTER EXPLORES the possibility of a co-productive inter-generational relationship where parents and children co-produce creation, a loving context for the process of transforming of the universe. Inspired by MeShell Ndegeocello's "Solomon," I contextualize this transformation of the meaning of creation within Audre Lorde's lesbian feminist politics of mothering and offer it as a transformative critique of the norms of Hip-Hop discourse. This chapter, much like Ndegeocello's song, is a journey.

First we will discuss the queer potential of Black mothering as a methodology for revaluing Black life in the contemporary social landscape, shaped by the criminalization of mothering through the policing function of so-called social services, and then we will walk through the complexity of Ndegeocello's piece, finally connecting it to a Black feminist tradition of transforming the meaning of masculinity by linking Ndegeocello's cosmology of creation and light to Audre Lorde's vision for her son's participation in our collective liberation as described in her 1979 essay "Manchild," and her 1984 essay "Turning the Beat Around:

Lesbian Parenting 1984." Lorde's concept of the beat and the necessity of turning it around resonates, with the Hip-Hop methodology I employ in this chapter. It invokes both the economically and socially violent circumstances that have made Hip-Hop necessary and salient, as well as the violent attitudes against women latent in mainstream manifestations of Hip-Hop culture.

MOTHERING AS A RADICAL THREAT

If we acknowledge that Hip-Hop was a cry from Black and Latino youth, screaming against the common knowledge that they were not supposed to exist, we have to ask ourselves about the birth process that made those creative screams possible. We also have to remember that Hip-Hop was born in the era when politicians (including Ronald Reagan) made careers from the criminalization of young women of color for the act of giving birth (Roberts 1998: 8). Remember that before Hip-Hop became a scapegoat for everything—violence, low-scholastic achievement, uncontainable sexuality and general "bad behavior"—young, poor and racialized mothers were already blamed for being the primary reproducers of a "culture of poverty" (Lewis 2).[1] Before conservatives in the United States began to mobilize to censor and criminalize Hip-Hop, they had already convened to prevent the dangerous creative act of mothering by women of color.

For example, Gary Bauer, chief aide to Ronald Reagan, and a proponent of abortion and sterilization targeted at poor women, said that because of their "reckless choices," "there will either be no next generation, or a next generation that is worse than none at all" (Solinger 194). In 1977, Richard Rosenthal of the World Bank suggested that a quarter of the women in developing nations should be sterilized to prevent economically disruptive revolutions (Rodriguez 1). As Gwendolyn Mink points out in *Welfare's End*, in the 1990s 72 percent of mothers on welfare had two children or less and 61 percent never had more children while on welfare (Mink 75). The slew of policies and media slanders of poor mothers leading up to the effective dismantling of welfare in the United States was based on stereotypes, a particular form of repetitive storytelling practiced by politicians in the United States.

It is important to remember that this hyper-criminalization of the reproductive capacity of poor women and women of color is its own story, not based on facts, but rather based on the terms of a narrative of a particular version of neoliberal capitalism. This version promotes a society where life, food, housing, and education, among other basic needs and rights, are individual problems and not community concerns. As Patricia Hill Collins points out in *Black Feminist Thought*, the criminalization of Black mothers "diverts attention from the political and economic inequality affecting Black mothers and children and suggests that anyone can rise from poverty if he or she only received good values at home" (Collins 74). Like Hip-Hop, the love of poor and racialized mothers has never been trusted to teach values that will train young people up into conformity with capitalism and consent to a political system that continually exploits and disenfranchises the communities they come from.

I find it useful to talk about the myth of poor and racialized mothers as "welfare queens" (Reagan's phrase), as an example of what Wahnee-ma Lubiano calls a "cover story" (Lubiano 323). Just like actions to censor Hip-Hop and devalue it as a creative form stem from fear of the truthful critiques that many Hip-Hop artists are launching, the story of the deviant and dangerous mother is only necessary because of one transformative truth: mothers of color, queer mothers, poor mothers and radical mothers are changing the meaning of life everyday just by the value and attention they give to the growth of knowledge and ways of living that cannot be contained by capitalism. Unfortunately, the fact that Hip-Hop and queer mothering are both criminalized by the same terms and often by the same people does not mean that Hip-Hop discourse does not participate in the disciplining and devaluing of the subjectivity of Black mothers. I will not rehearse the catalog of songs that assert (like opponents of welfare) that gold-digging women have babies in order trick men and get money, that Black mothers are to blame for everything that goes wrong in life, that a Black mother is inadequate to the task of raising a "man," and so on. The saddest part is that even the depictions of motherhood that idealize the mother as a strong figure, responsible for saving the lives of countless rappers, are still dehumanizing, participating in a dichotomy very similar to the dominant narrative where a woman is either an asexual, eternal strong, unquestioningly supportive version of the virgin Mary, or an expendable scheming whore in the figure of Eve.

The status of the mother within the Hip-Hop lexicon is not new. It is not only influenced by a dominant western virgin/whore dichotomy, but it is also an inheritance from the way some aspects of the cultural nationalist strain of the Black Power movement consented to a patriarchal perspective on the status of women. I find it useful to invoke Audre Lorde's work here to reveal the violent implications of the status of women in the absence of accountability in a male-centered narrative about the meaning of Black life and Black communities. Mothering, like Hip-Hop, was part of a creative response to the Reagan era's insistence that some lives, in particular African-American, Afro-Caribbean and Latino lives in the United States, were worthless. Mothering, and in particular radical practices and affirmations of Black mothering, or what I understand to be practices of nurturing the exploited, the criminalized, the undervalued, the sacrificed, the sacred, the immeasurable, the magical within ourselves and each other intergenerationally, demonstrate what it means to create something from anything, insisting on an alternate meaning and mode of living. Life can mean more than what oppression lets us have.

In this sense, I argue that there is a way of reading the activity of mothering as queer in the context of Hip-Hop, where the dominant mode of engagement is a hyper-masculine fetishization of access to capitalist trophies and misogynistic control of women. Pin-balling between the dehumanizing criminalization of the "gold-digger" and the also dehumanizing reverence for the sacrificial "dear mama," the queer practices of mothering (practices that threaten the reproduction of the status quo by passionately exceeding the normatively defined limits of love) that change the meaning of life are only visible in the fissures of the Hip-Hop narrative.

The cost of the valorization of the most violent and exploitative versions of masculinity within dominant iterations of Hip-Hop is complicit in the ongoing violence against Black women in mainstream society. Within Black communities, the transformative potential of Hip-Hop to overthrow the system of capitalist and patriarchal violence that made it necessary as a form of radical self-expression to begin with has also been lost. But there is another story that can be told here. This chapter looks at the ways that queer articulations of mothering from Audre Lorde to MeShell Ndegeocello speak within a Black feminist context and through Hip-Hop to critique harmful norms of Black masculinity.

I.

ALL CREATION: MESHELL NDEGEOCELLO
AND THE METAPHYSICS OF SHINE

Black mothering is a queer thing. Here queer means everything that challenges the reproduction of a dominant narrative about what life means. And in this stage of late capitalism in the United States, the dominant narrative is that Black mothering decreases the value of life in general. As Cathy Cohen argues in "Punks, Bulldaggers and Welfare Queens: Towards a Queer Politics?" those categories of living that read as "queer" in the social narrative often exceed the scope of gay, lesbian or bisexual sexual identities and include those people whose sexual, household or love and life making behavior is criminalized by the state (Cohen 465). Jasbir Puar's *Terrorist Assemblages* follows Cohen's assertion to examine how racialized so-called terrorists are queered by the state's perception of the danger of what they might reproduce, at the same time that self-identified gays and lesbians claim more citizenship rights (Puar 5).

My use of the term queer is influenced by this theoretical trajectory and also by my work as a queer organizer for social justice with organizations such as Southerners on New Ground, an intersectional queer liberation organization led by working class queers of all backgrounds. Our definition of queer liberation is informed by economic justice, racial justice and immigration justice politics and acknowledges that our queerness exceeds our sexual practices and includes a passionate insistence that the interconnection of our lives and the interdependence of all forms of life on the planet inform our social world. In my work I point out that this insistence on interdependence manifests in Black feminist literary and cultural tradition under the terminology of "mothering."[2] As Hortense Spillers argues in "Mama's Baby, Papa's Maybe: A New American Grammar Book," in the history of Black women in the United States, specifically under slavery, "motherhood" denotes the status and privilege under patriarchy that Black women have legally and discursively been denied, while "mothering" refers to the labor of nurturing that can be extracted from enslaved and economically oppressed women on behalf of privileged children (through the labor of mammies and nannies).

My work explores the ways that this labor of mothering can also be used queerly, in ways that exceed and threaten a capitalist hetero-patriarchal structure. Dorothy Roberts' work in "Feminism Race and Adoption" (2006) and *Shattered Bonds* (2009) exposes the history of the criminalization of Black mothers and the ways the contemporary actions of state social services continue the project of chattel slavery to disrupt the bonds between Black people and the children they choose to mother.[3] Therefore, I take MeShell Ndegeocello's work to reference a cosmology that affirms Black life as a spiritual practice of planetary love, as a work of queer mothering. In order to do this transformative work of reframing the value of Black life and the meaning of parenting, Ndegeocello's "Solomon" engages the discourse of "shine" a term within Hip-Hop discourse that navigates the relationship between capitalist accumulation and Black self-worth.

In Hip-Hop discourse "shine" is a noun, a verb, a proper noun, a quality and an aspiration. Usually in the Hip-Hop lexicon "shine" refers to the apparent wealth of the speaker, their attractiveness, their diamond to skin ratio, or their lyrical skill. Bigger than "bling," shine usually reflects a more profound aura or at least more generally admirable quality. Some Hip-Hop artists claim to out "shine" the competition. Some Hip-Hop artists reverse the pseudo parental slight insult of the colloquialism "son" (often used to suggest that the speaker is more experienced and knowledgeable than the addressee) in order to reflect the inner shine of their peers, or as Raekwon explains: "I call my brother Sun 'cause he shines like one" (Raekwon, Chorus). Having already deeply explored the cosmological symbolism of this on her intergalactic love album *Comfort Woman*, MeShell Ndegeocello reframes the discourse of "Shine" within Hip-Hop masculinity on her seventh album, *The World Has Made Me the Man of My Dreams*, which in its title suggests that she has a personal stake in a queer relationship to the social meanings of masculinity. The song titled "Solomon" (root Sol—as in Sun), referencing the biblical King, brings the bright potential of the name "Sun" back into the intergenerational relationship in a song that she offers "for my son."[4] A listener familiar with the story of the mother who faces the prospect of giving up her child in order to save him from being cut in half (as is the case in the biblical story in which Solomon mediates the claim of two women to the same child)—also the case in the impact of "child welfare" policies that consider splitting up families to be in the best interest of poor and Black children—might intuit that Ndegeocello's offering of advice and spiritual context for her son speaks both to the discourse of the embattled, criminalized Black mother and to the debate on who and what is valuable within Hip-Hop discourse.

Ndegeocello describes herself as influenced by Hip-Hop among other Black musical forms, but she is just as compellingly engaged in the contemporary critical and art movement that engages Hip-Hop as a language through which to create transformative and accessible Black cultural critique. Her collaboration with Greg Tate, in the liner notes and art for her 1993 album *Plantation Lullabies*, exemplifies how while not conforming to the norms of Hip-Hop practitioners, Ndegeocello sees Hip-Hop as part of a legacy of rhythmic Black transformative speech and an opportunity for intergenerational and broad discursive intervention. So while no track on *The World Has Made Me the Man of My Dreams* reproduced the classic emcee stance interspersed with funky bass guitar that Ndegeocello provides on "If That's Your Boyfriend He Wasn't Last Night" off *Plantation Lullabies*, Ndegeocello continues to use rhythmic talking with and through rhythm, this time in the form of prayer, to transform the listeners, the topics she engages and the limits of what Hip-Hop can be.

Ndegeocello takes on a complete transformation of the process through which the universe, relationships and people are recreated, transcending and challenging normative narratives about what parenting means, especially the criminalization of Black parenting. This intervention into the meaning of Black parenting beyond the normative boundaries of gender is part of the work of Black mothering. By including the perspective of what it means to be a father at the beginning of the piece, and by referring to her own parenting in gender neutral terms, Ndegeocello participates in a practice of queer mothering enacted by people of multiple genders in oppressed Black communities. Just as Hortense Spillers notes that the work of mothering for enslaved "women" was separated from the status of womanhood, I consider Black mothering a queer practice, a form of subversive labor that Black people who are house mothers in Black gay ball culture, teachers in reconstruction era schoolhouses in the south, biological mothers, aunties, big mamas, siblings, mentors and others, have participated in for centuries. Therefore I name Ndegeocello's discursive participation in the Black feminist and queer practice of transforming the meaning of life, "Black mothering" even though her work impacts the revaluation of Black parenting in general.

Countering the reproduction of Blackness as abjection through the cultural criminalization of Black parenting, Ndegeocello offers a poetic possibility that nullifies the force of social reproduction with a space for what her song "Solomon" calls "all creation."

Ndegeocello's representation of herself as a parent is queered on a number of levels. Her own masculinity in relationship to mothering challenges the idea of fatherlessness that shapes much of the discourse on Black (single) mothering in the United States.[5] Ndegeocello's proclamation in the album title that "The World Has Made Me the Man of My Dreams" participates in a longer discourse through which Black single mothers have been challenging the definition of their families as "illegitimate" and "fatherless." For example, in the 1970s a Brooklyn-based organization called the Sisterhood of Black Single Mothers published this statement defining their own families:

> Not illegitimate: Regardless of the circumstances of a child's birth, he or she is here. To impose a negative label on a child is to say to that child that you do not expect much from them. Positive descriptions coupled with high expectations are key to motivating our children. Not fatherless: Simply stated, why define a household by who is not there? A family does not cease to exist because one parent isn't there. How about motherful? (Matin 52)

While countless Hip-Hop artists and single Black mothers recount the experience of being "both mother and father" to their children, their role is still often understood in the context of lack, where the mother ostensibly wishes that the man of her dreams would materialize and take on his share of the labor (if not ... more problematically ... his destined patriarchal role). For Ndegeocello however, the man of her dreams is already present. The world, or her range of experiences, lessons learned, and responsibilities have made her into that person who would and could fulfill her needs and by extension the needs of her son for an inspiring role model. In the context she creates in "Solomon" there is no lack. Only abundance. Ndegeocello uses voice samples, a reggae loop and the discourse of shine to make it clear that Hip-Hop, with its practice of looping other musical genres and sampled voices, is a technology of revaluing undervalued social practices, including Black parenting. Her intervention into the process of creation between parents and children, and mothers and sons in particular, provides a feminist context for Black masculinity, working towards the sustainability and vitality of Hip-Hop culture as a queer mothering practice.

But, what does this actually mean? What does it sound like? In the following section I examine how Ndegeocello manifests this in the song itself and the questions it raises before delving into its relationship to the tradition of Black feminist mothering as an intervention into the reproduction of dominant masculinity.

II.
SOLOMON

We hear a young man speaking.

"*Only you have made my bad days turn good.*"

He must be talking about his mother, because who else knows how to unconditionally love a young Black man in America?

"*You was the one that put a smile on my face. You was the one that I knew I could always come to when I was down and know...*"

Who else accepts co-responsibility for transforming all of those "bad days" imposed on a young Black man into a livable reality? Who else would dare provide refuge from a state system that targets them and then seeks to throw them away into prison or the cemetery?

"*...when I saw you in the crib. I'd have a smile again. I thank Most High for you.*"

In the crib? Is this a Hip-Hop colloquialism? Crib as dwelling place? Or has our speaker flipped the script? Does all the power for transformation and comfort reside in a child?

"*'Cause without you I don't know what I would do. Man I feel good just to be father. To be a father man, it's no better feeling in the world.*"

Maybe both. Maybe there is a hidden relationship to mothering that enables the speaker to find deep joy and accountability in being a father.

This is where the music comes in.

"*And I have to do my part to make sure that you have a part. I know that to be true. I love you. I thank Most High for you every day. That you're mines.*"

Who is this young man? And then like Saturn's ring turned slingshot we are warned that the bass is ready. A deep and familiar voice. The artist MeShell Ndegeocello makes her concise claim:

"*For my son.*"

In contrast to what we might have expected to be the run of the mill Hip-Hop song, or at best the "proud baby daddy" interlude on an otherwise violent album, MeShell Ndegeocello makes space for a spiritually rich gender/queer feminist intervention. We are transported; beamed up into a cosmic reggae paradise where Bob Marley rides shooting stars. Ndegeocello is whispering insistently "Shine," like we are stars ready to be born, moonflower seeds in need of motivation to push through the driest ground. This is an injunction and a reminder. A Command: "Shine." The universe is vibrant around us. We are possible. The artist speaks to us in her own voice on two registers—in chorus a sung offering and in a spoken teaching/prayer that immediately follows the articulated offering:

> Offering: *All. I. Am.*
> Teaching: *Flesh and blood, I've been blessed to feed myself*
> *with the creations from my mind and hands; God has blessed me.*
> *The sun that shines. Shine for me. Ha.*
> Offering: *Bless me. Shine for me. Shine for me. May you never*
> *be lonely, no.*
> Teaching: *My mother and father, my vessel to this blessed earth.*
> *I thank you for my life.*
> Offering: *I thank you for my life.*
> Teaching: *All praises due as the creator of all things true. I thank*
> *you for my life.*
> Offering: *I thank you for my life.*
> Teaching: *And I praise you.*

Who is the audience for the multi-vocal invocation? Praise who? God? Thank who? All parents, partners with the universe in creation? The sun? The son? The child? The young father whose voice we just heard? Ndegeocello co-parents with herself here. Creating balance and reinforcing lessons. Becoming mother and father. Becoming a vessel for what? What does it mean to never be lonely? Does this require a self-sustained multiplicity? How do we cultivate the intimacy with nature, with self, with cosmos, with each other that would allow us to never be lonely?

"God has blessed me," she states. Are blessings natural? Is it possible that one would be able to feed themselves from their own passionate creations? It is certainly a rare situation in the context of capitalism where making a living and making life often seem at odds. The space cradle rock-a-bye of the song continues. The praise offering continues. The gratitude continues and over it, we receive a lesson about how the things of the world come and go. The refrain shifts to "all creation," creating a robust audience that includes all life, and all matter as beloved creations, and participants in the process of creation. In her words: "Flowers. Trees. Birds. Fish. Me. You." Parents.

III.

In her article "Like an Old Soul Record: Black Feminism, Queer Sexuality, and the Hip Hop Generation," Andreana Clay contextualizes MeShell Ndegeocello's queer self-presentation in the terms of Black feminist theorists, including Audre Lorde, suggesting that Ndegeocello's relevance to Hip-Hop is as generational as it is generic, if not more (2007: 53). I affirm this contextualization and participate in it, offering Audre Lorde's theorizations of radical Black lesbian feminist parenting as precedents and partners that enable and support the revised context of creation that Ndegeocello inhabits and invites us into with "Solomon," as a musician circulating in the cultural era dominated by Hip-Hop, but also as a mother who pays attention to whether her son watches booty-shaking music videos (http://www.youtube.com/watch?v=q9x6v-0hmXg). Audre Lorde's essay "Man Child:: A Black Lesbian Feminist's Response," is her most well known theorization of parenting, particularly on the subject of raising a son. In the original publication in *Conditions*, a feminist literary journal, a large subheading/pull quote emphasizes Lorde's statement that she is speaking "not only of relationship but of relating" (1979: 30). This indicates that parenting, for Lorde, is a process, a continual set of actions, a dynamic possibility. In fact, as Lorde clarifies in the essay, the crystallization of the mother-son relationship that is often required by dominant society is deadly. Lorde resists this norm by "teaching my son that I do not exist to do his feeling for him" (1979: 31). As Lorde elaborates in this essay, patriarchy functions in part to outsource the labor of feeling to women, leaving men to be unfeeling. Of course this idea of unfeeling men is harmful not only to men who are encouraged to repress their own emotions, but to everyone who experiences the violent behavior that often results from emotional repression.

One explanation for the tendencies within Hip-Hop to turn feminization into an insult, using homophobia and violent language to assert dominance, would be the mandate to equate the lack of feeling or empathy with power. This manifests in many forms; the use of female R&B singers or samples to express an emotional refrain, leaving an emcee free to contradict or evade the motivations for their own songs; the often over-stated emphasis on NOT loving women in mainstream Hip-Hop; and the reservation of one tentatively allowed soft spot for the "Dear Mama" who has ideally taken on the emotional labor that neither father nor son will indulge. Lorde's commitment in parenting is instructive:

> I wish to raise a Black man who will not be destroyed by, nor settle for those corruptions called power by the white fathers who mean his destruction as surely as they mean mine. I wish to raise a Black man who will recognize that the legitimate objects of his hostility are not women, but the particulars of a structure that programs him to fear and despise women as well as his own Black self. (Lorde 1979: 74)

Lorde's intention for her own son could be a missive to the Hip-Hop generation. And it is also a sentiment shared by many mothers who raise sons in partnership with the formative influence of Hip-Hop. Listen to Lorde's observation with mainstream music video versions of Hip-Hop in mind: "Men who are afraid to feel must keep women around to do their feeling for them while dismissing us for the same supposedly 'inferior' capacity" (Lorde 1979: 74). How, then, do those of us who want to mother in a way that allows men access to their own emotions where they would love themselves and others, go about doing this? Lorde's work is instructive in content as well in form.

Lorde offers her own strategy in "Man Child." She intends to give her son the power to experience his own emotions by looking deeply within herself at the ways she interacts with him. Examining her own constructions of masculinity as violence (for example when her son is beat up by a bully) she strives to recognize her own fear that her son will be hurt. Instead of avoiding it by trying to turn him into an unfeeling, indestructible robot, she gives herself permission to show him her own emotions of fear, her experiences of being bullied, revealing the fact that she is a parent and partner with him, not a God who already knows it all already. She explains that:

The strongest lesson I can teach my son is the same lesson I teach my daughter: how to be who he wishes to be for himself. And the best way I can do this is to be who I am and hope that he will learn from this not how to be me, which is not possible, but how to be himself. (1979: 77)

Ndegeocello models this approach by dedicating the song "Solomon" to her son. Suggesting that her son, like the sun, has a cosmic role in the universe, she models an ethical relationship by expressing her own gratitude and reverence for her life and all life.

Though Audre Lorde's essays have not been set to music, there is also something musical about Lorde's approach to lesbian parenting. In 1984 in a lesser known essay published in a now out of print collection called *Burst of Light* and now reprinted in the new anthology of Lorde's work *I Am Your Sister*, Lorde characterizes lesbian parenting as "Turning the Beat Around," by invoking the idea of beat to represent the violent repetitive tendencies that literally beat down and kill people of color and gay and lesbian people all over the world. She positions lesbian parenting as an intervention into a violent status quo which includes hate, violence, lack of access to healthcare, divestment from social services, imperialism, and homophobia.

I invoke Lorde's idea of the "beat" to mean the feedback loop reproducing a particular meaning of life where the lives of communities of color, queer communities and poor communities are made expendable, literally through beating us down with state and economic violence. The "beat" also operates on an interpersonal level, allowing internalized racism and classism, combined with a logic that devalues the autonomy and agency of women to lead to a common sense of violence against women and girls, people of color and queer people in each of these communities, that reproduces the logic of a dominant society that hates us. In 1984 Lorde was using the popular culture recognition of Paula Abdul's "Turning the Beat Around" to describe her process of revising the meaning of life, just as decades later MeShell Ndegeocello uses the discourse of "shine" to make her project legible to a Hip-Hop fluent audience. Lorde calls on her 1984 audience and all of us as partners in creation, on the level of rhythm and interpersonal relationships. Ndegeocello and all creation answer the call in chorus when we realize the pricelessness of all of our living, and shine.

CONCLUSION

The project of turning the beat around is not finished, it is ongoing. It is the soundtrack to our intergenerational multi-gendered conversation. It is Hip-Hop. It is how we have turned cheap and stolen house paint into street murals. It is how we will turn bling into blessings, it is how we shine all over ourselves and each other without the need to exploit or dominate anyone. In her act to create a cosmic space of abundance and love for Black parents, MeShell Ndegeocello is the man of Audre Lorde's dreams and the purveyor of the Hip-Hop incarnation of the practice of queer Black mothering—the active and lived revision of the meaning of life. Play the song for your son, for your daughter, for your gender/queer students, for yourself radiating into the rhythm we deserve.

[1]Oscar Lewis coined the term "culture of poverty" in his 1959 anthropological study *Five Families: Mexican Case Studies in the Culture of Poverty*. In his introduction Lewis generalized the phenomenon, which he constructed from his observations of five families in one part of Mexico to apply to people living in poverty across regional and national borders. While he cited studies to back up his application of the culture of poverty to poor people in London and Puerto Rico, he offered no citation for his application of this phenomenon to "lower class Negroes in the United States" (2).

[2]See Gumbs.

[3]See Roberts 2006 and 2009.

[4]To see Ndegeocello talk about sexual politics in music and society from her vantage point as the parent of a 20-year-old son see: <http://www.youtube.com/watch?v=q9x6v-0hmXg>. Zen Cat Productions, 2009. Accessed 1/5/2012.

[5]The representation of this fear of fatherlessness that has had the most social and political impact is Daniel P. Moynihan's *The Negro Family: The Case for National Action*. Also known as "The Moynihan Report" this piece of policy recommendation is a treatise that explains the economic and social problems of Black Americans as a result of mother-led households. The impact of the report was to justify policies that denied resources to single mothers.

WORKS CITED

Clay, Andreana. "Like an Old Soul Record: Black Feminism, Queer Sexuality, and the Hip-Hop Generation." *Meridians: feminism, race transnationalism* 8.1 (2007): 53-73.

Cohen, Cathy. "Punks, Bulldaggers, and Welfare Queens: The Radical Potential of Queer Politics?" *Gay and Lesbian Quarterly* 3.4 (1997): 437-65.

Collins, Patricia Hill. *Black Feminist Thought*. New York: Routledge, 1991.

Gumbs, Alexis Pauline. "We Can Learn to Mother Ourselves: A Dialogically Produced Audience and Black Feminist Publishing 1979 to the Present." *Gender Forum: An Internet Journal for Gender Studies* 22 (2008). Web. <http://www.genderforum.org/index.php?id=170>.

Lewis, Oscar. *Five Families: Mexican Case Studies in the Culture of Poverty*. New York: Basic Books, 1959.

Lorde, Audre. "Turning the Beat Around: Lesbian Parenting 1984." *A Burst of Light*. Ithaca, NY: Firebrand Books, 1988. 39-48.

Lorde, Audre. *Sister Outsider*. San Francisco: Spinsters Ink, 1985.

Lorde, Audre. "Man Child: A Black Lesbian Feminist's Response." *Conditions* 4 (1979): 30-36.

Lubiano, Wahneema. "Black Ladies, Welfare Queens, and State Minstrels: Ideological War by Narrative Means." *Race-ing Justice, Engendering Power: The Anita Hill-Clarence Thomas Controversy and the Construction of Social Reality*. Ed. Toni Morrison. New York: Pantheon Books, 1992. 323-363.

Matin, Khadihah. "Adolescent Pregnancy: The Perspective of the Sisterhood of Black Single Mothers," *Journal of Community Health* 11.1 (1986): 49-53.

Mink, Gwendolyn. *Welfare's End*. New York: New York University Press, 1999.

Moynihan, Daniel P. *The Negro Family: The Case for National Action*. Washington, DC: Office of Policy Planning and Research. United States Department of Labor, 1965.

Ndegeocello, MeShell. *The World Has Made Me the Man of My Dreams*. Emarcy, 2007.

Puar, Jaspir K. *Terrorist Assemblages: Homonationalism in Queer Times*. Durham, Duke University Press, 2007.

Raekwon. "Wu-Gambinos." *Only Build 4 Cuban Linx*. Loud Records, 1995.

Roberts, Dorothy. *Killing the Black Body: Race, Reproduction and the Meaning of Liberty*, New York: Vintage, 1998.

Roberts, Dorothy. "Feminism Race and Adoption." *The Color of Violence*. Eds. INCITE. Cambridge, MA: South End Press, 2006. 42-52.

Roberts, Dorothy. *Shattered Bonds: The Color of Child Welfare.* New York: Perseus Books, 2009.

Rodriguez, Luz. "Population Control in Puerto Rico." Conference Presentation at *Let's Talk About Sex*, the SisterSong 10th Anniversary Conference, 31 May-3 June 2007, Chicago, IL.

Solinger. Rickie. *Beggars and Choosers: How the Politics of Choice Shapes Adoption, Abortion and Welfare in the United States.* New York: Hill and Wang, 2001.

Spillers, Hortense. "Mama's Baby, Papa's Maybe: A New American Grammar Book." *African American Literary Theory: A Reader.* Ed. Winston Napier. New York: New York University Press, 2000.

5.
360 Degrees

RUTH HENRY (MC OASIS)

I

Hip-Hop will knock you on your face/ just 2 see if u'll get up/
Hip-Hop will make u cry, will make u sweat, will make it tough/
Hip-Hop will make u prove u love it/in the bottom of yr soul/
Hip-Hop will tear u to pieces n Hip-Hop will make u whole....

I HAD BEEN LIVING in Colombia for five days when I found out I was
pregnant with my first daughter. The woman that my yearlong community arts grant had assigned me to stay with, Rosalba, couldn't
figure out why I kept puking in the mornings. She assured me she only
used bottled water, had even washed the vegetables with it. Where could I
have gotten the parasites? She was worried sick. I was fresh off the plane
from Boston, my home. Couldn't believe I'd finally made it to Colombia,
a trip I'd had in mind for the past five years ever since I learned that
the U.S. was mixed up in massacres here, similar to the ones I'd seen
the after-effects of at age nineteen in Guatemala. At first I'd planned to
come as an international observer to one of the peace communities, but
my mother had been scared sick, and we'd made a deal: I'd apply for a
Fulbright grant, and if I got it, she'd get off my case. Of course, now she
loves the place, and comes to visit my family and I here a couple times
a year ... but I am getting ahead of myself. In 2002, during a typically
cloudy week in Bogotá, all I could do was try to keep my breakfast down
and hope my stomach bug would pass quickly so I could get out and do
the work I'd come to do.

On day five, I figured it was time to go to the clinic. Bob Marley's classic
"No Woman No Cry" seeped through my headphones, lucky stone in

71

my pocket. I was, as I would be for much of my first pregnancy, alone. After reading *positivo* over and over again on the small blue paper, I was tempted to tell the receptionist something, anything. Something like: Holy shit. I just got here. All I know about your country is there's supposed to be this crazy civil war going on. I've heard my country is involved in it somehow. I have no one here. This baby's father is back in Boston, and he doesn't even know where he'll be living this month. He doesn't even have a phone. Me? I'm here to study art. I miss my mom. She's the one who passed art on to me, ever since I was a kid. This journal I've been scribbling in while I wait? Oh, well, I'm a poet. And MC. And I'm scared. But this was Bogotá. There was already a long line behind me, and the receptionist looked like she had had a hard day. I turned up my Walkman and walked in a haze out onto the street. Bus fumes mingled with the smell of fresh arepas.[1] I held tight to my lucky stone.

The next three months passed in a blur. I couldn't get in touch with my daughter's father, though I knew the grapevine or my letters had reached him. He'd called one morning while I was in class then never called back. I was getting sick every time I heard the phone ring, spending too much time tucked under blankets, doing nothing. The art courses my grant had set me up for were at a high-class university where I felt totally out of place, and friend making was going at a snail's pace. Not to mention the fact that most of the time my stomach felt like a bulldozer high on coke, tearing down the Berlin Wall while dancing the samba. So when we got a chance to take a week's vacation from school, I took a fellow grantee's advice and headed for Hotel Bella Vista in Cartagena.

Some moments in life feel like magic. Maybe they are. Or maybe they're not. My daughter says love is magic. My cousin says coincidence is an eleven-letter word for God. All I know is, my life turned both upside down and downside up that week. And then I found Hip-Hop, and with it, found my footing. Echoes in this far off land, of the community I had built for myself in Boston over the last few years, of the mix-matched batch of poets and artists and Hip-Hop heads that had gathered for interminable jam sessions in my shared Jamaica Plain apartment. Deep thump of bass and teasing chase of rhyme suddenly as comforting as a lullaby swathed in soft moonlight. As my mother singing me to sleep through a telephone receiver in her off tune voice while I'd curled in blue blankets of college dorm heartbreak a few years earlier. Comforting as the smell of old books filled with my father's pencil-marked revelations in his basement study at

the Watertown house I grew up in. As finding my journal the day after
I'd lost it while traveling alone through Egypt, hugging it to my chest
like a lover rescued from a fire. Hip-Hop. Reminiscent of stumbling on
an empty synagogue while backpacking through Morocco, feeling my
grandmother in the Hebrew letters of an old prayer book.

Hotel Bella Vista is indeed a hotel, but there are many people who live
there for years, paying monthly rent and packing their stuff up come
December to make room for the flood of tourists whose money keeps
the hotel afloat for the rest of the next year, when the regulars come
back to their rooms. It is an old, sprawling one floor wonderland full of
white pillars and draping begonias. In the communal kitchen strangers
get to know each other, and in the central patio people find lifelong
friends. Which is where I met Eva Maria, a young dreamer with bright
blue contacts that shocked against the cinnamon of her skin. She gave
workshops on how to run a community radio station in a neighborhood
called Nelson Mandela, on the outskirts of Cartagena. I don't remember
how we got to talking about Hip-Hop, but she invited me to come with
her one-day and meet with some of the young MCs there.

The Nelson Mandela *barrio*² is what's called over here an invasion.
This means that families funnel in from other parts of the country,
displaced by the violence of the civil war, and take over some no man's
land, mounting shacks out of cardboard, wood, tin, whatever they can
get. Nelson Mandela has been around for a while, and in the older sections of the barrio there are plenty of fully constructed houses. On the
ever-expanding edges are shacks. As we drove down a muddy dirt road
to get there, Eva Maria told me that things were kind of tense in the
barrio lately, that the youth would probably be happy for a fresh face,
something new to do and think about. Two weeks earlier the Grupo de
Limpieza Social (Social Cleansing Group) had left the corpses of a couple
of fifteen-year-old trouble starters on the side of the road as a warning.

If I'd known about the social cleansing groups then as I do now, as
does anyone who's spent time in Colombia's poorer neighborhoods, then
perhaps I wouldn't have been so surprised by what happened next. We
got out at the entrance to Nelson Mandela and walked through the mud
towards a group of people huddled around the neighborhood's main
building. Eva asked a group of little girls on the outskirts of the throng
what was going on. A sign had been posted on the wall. Thirty-six names.
Forty-eight hours to pack up and leave town for good, or be killed where

and whenever they were found. The names, as I saw for myself once the crowd thinned out, were first names, nicknames even. Later, as I sat on the porch with one of the youth leaders Eva Maria introduced me to, he explained that this was a scare tactic. You never know exactly whom they're targeting. "They say it's just for delinquents," he explained, "but sometimes it's community leaders like me. They get the lists from the police," he said. "Or the paramilitaries. Then they do their dirty work." As he walked me down the street to meet some MCs, he wondered out loud if he would pack up that night. His name, Juan, had been on the list, but then, there were so many Juans...

What did I know of Social Cleansing Groups, of paramilitaries and civil wars? Why did a spooky wave of familiarity rush over me? Certainly this was nothing I'd seen in Watertown, nor in Jamaica Plain. But five years earlier, writing my college thesis in post civil war Guatemala, I'd gotten a deep, bitter taste. I'd gone for six months, inspired by a close friend who'd been born there. Studied Spanish intensively, then headed for the mountains, then the coast, and then the jungle. I'd swallowed stories of massacre survivors, visions of mass graves exhumed in a pile of small haunting bones. Then swigged them down with history books that outlined my own country's role in the genocide of 700 indigenous villages, razed to the ground in the name of cheap bananas. I tried to write about it, draw about it, but then felt the strange guilt of handing it over to my professors, who I knew would do nothing more with these terrible stories than grade them. It was a nun named Eva who I met in one of the communities of massacre survivors there, CPR Primavera Ix-can, that set me on my path to Colombia. She'd visited and seen history repeating itself. In Guatemala I'd never heard of social cleansing groups, but I'd heard plenty of civil patrols, and the parallel sent chills up my spine. What, I wondered to myself, was my homeland mixed up in this time? All those taxes they took out of my ESOL teacher paycheck: where did the money go? What were they financing?

I followed Juan to a round stone circle where a couple of the MCs sat waiting. We shared rhymes back and forth. Mine choked on the greed of the land I'd been born in, spat it back up in questions that snagged on the edge of a silent beat and swayed there, halted on their journey towards an answer. Theirs skipped over and past the beat, down dusty streets towards one-room houses with *sancocho*[3] on the stove and a great grandmother caught in her grandson's throat. They introduced me to Raga, a deep throated branch off somewhere between Hip-Hop and reggae. I introduced them to Spoken Word. Then after lunch they took me to a small shack where a group of local musicians were rehearsing. In the jam session that followed, the fearless honesty with which they freestyled about that morning's list, about the links between the social cleansing groups and the police, and about their own refusal to keep quiet had me covered in goosebumps. Back home in Boston, corrupt cops were a bitch, and sure, we all rhymed about fucked up searches ... but at least they didn't send out vigilante groups to chop youth to pieces! I was a sobbing wreck that night at the hotel. The waves crashed outside against the yellow rocks, mocking the steady storm of my own tears, where I flailed my arms and held onto Hip-Hop for dear life. I didn't want the sadness to take over and seep into my womb. I needed it to be my anchor.

Sometimes our prayers are answered quicker than we can even form them. That weekend a group of people from the hotel invited me to go with them to the Annual Drum Festival in Palenque de San Basilio. Palenque was the first liberated territory in the Americas, autonomous ever since it was founded by Benkus Bohio and the other runaway slaves who followed him out of Cartagena and into the woods. In the middle of the plaza Bohio's statue looms larger than life, fist raised at the sky, chains broken, mouth open in a cry of eternal defiance. The Palenqueros who live there today stem from this original group, and they hold stubbornly to African traditions long lost to most of the Diaspora. They have their own language, a Creole between the mixed African dialects of their predecessors and Spanish. They also have their own system of communal governance, autonomous from the rest of the nation. And the annual drum festival. There is a regular stage during the day, full of music and dance. But by night, everyone parades through the dirt roads with drums and lanterns. Pounding my feet against the ground, I felt strength returning to me there, encircling my womb and holding it firm.

And then I met Fusion Latina—four young MCs from Cartagena spitting about their pride in their African roots on the main stage under a blaring sun. KP/Ruzza, who today rhymes with me in our female Hip-Hop collective, El Matriarkao, was still just a toothpick of a girl then, tee shirt tucked up to show her midriff, bandana wrapped around her head. Rapping out the lyrics Fran had written for her, her own notebooks still gathering dust. But I didn't know that yet. I congratulated them on their set, introduced myself, and then on the way back to Cartagena piled in alongside them on the bus. A bunch of the other performers packed in too, tight like a box of crayons, and we freestyled the whole two-hour ride back to Cartagena. Many were stuck standing up, but everyone piled on laps when the bus driver warned us we were passing through a checkpoint. It was on that ride that someone told me about La HeroiK, a Hip-Hop movement in Cartagena, then at its apex, unifying around fifty Hip-Hop artists who met three times a week in the public library to practice their art forms. Hearing about La HeroiK, I knew I'd found the city where I wanted my daughter to be born.

II

Hip-Hop will be your refuge/ when the rest of the world rejects you/ n when u choose 2 rebel/ Hip-Hop will be right next 2 u/ Hip-Hop will climb yr spine/ will wind time inside a rhyme/ Hip-Hop will let the beat drop in the madness of yr mind

When I got back to Bogotá, a week later than I'd planned, I started the paperwork right away to get my grant moved to Cartagena. As I waited for the new semester to make the switch, I moved out of Rosalba's into a small room in the steep hilled bohemian neighborhood of Candelaria. A couple who roomed in the same house as I had a magazine, *Regeneraccion*, and as we got to know each other they suggested I cover Hip- Hop al Parque for them, Colombia's largest Hip-Hop festival, and the second largest in South America. I was on it!

At the concert, act after act blew my mind. This was so different from the Hip-Hop I knew back home, lifetimes away from the bullshit that had looped over and over again on the car radio, lifetimes away too from the gangsta rhymes I'd hear on the corner, detailing explicitly with sharp hitting punch lines the many ways a given MC would murder someone from another hood where they'd fallen into a decade-old beef. In Boston, there are some wonderful Hip-Hop artists, people who keep it real and keep it fresh and keep you thinking about what the hell is going on around us and what we can do to switch it up. But they are the minority, a small whisper against the booming speakers of the mainstream madness. In Colombia it is the other way around: you can find a little bit of everything, but the vast majority of the Hip-Hop artists out here are breaking down real experience with the lyricism of poets and the analysis of sociologists. The gangster bullshit and the bling-bling fame chasers are the minority, and they usually don't last too long on a big stage; the rest of the Hip-Hop community takes care of booing the bullshit off.

Thanks to the press pass my new housemates had hooked me up with, I got to go backstage during the festival and interview the artists into my little Walkman. Which is where I started getting schooled on what Colombian Hip-Hop was all about. It was also where I met Sepia, two girls whose presence on the stage had the set the whole 5000 deep crowd afire. The ladies are still one of my all time favorite Hip-Hop groups, though they are no longer together. It's been awhile since I spoke to them, but last I heard one got married and disappeared into motherhood and the other is still doing her thing, small scale. They said I should spend the Christmas break in their hometown of Cali, and check out the Hip-Hop scene there. So come December, I packed up, said goodbye to Bogotá, and set off for a new adventure. From Cali I would go straight on to Cartagena, have my baby and finish up my yearlong grant.

La Colonia. My first experience anywhere with an all female Hip-Hop collective. Sepia, it turned out, was just one of five or six groups that had come together for support 'n sisterhood in a largely masculine Hip-Hop culture. I was inspired off the bat. Together we watched Rachel Raimist's "Nobody Knows My Name," a documentary about female Hip-Hop artists, and vibed out reflecting on the challenges and benefits of being a young lady trying to get her voice respected in a sea of young men. Later, I would tell KP/Ruzza about La Colonia, and this would be the seed for us to start El Matriarkao, The Matriarchy. La Colonia has since split up. The challenges of juggling motherhood, the pressure from some of their husbands to leave rapping careers behind, got the better of it. But they inspired many of us, sent many seeds out to be sown.

By this point my belly was five months big, and the airline almost wouldn't let me fly to Cartagena. But I got here. And, as I'd hoped, I tracked down the library where La HeroiK met, and moved bit by bit into the Hip-Hop family that has helped to raise my daughter since the womb. Some nights the MCs would have the floor, sharing and refining lyrics, giving each other feedback or just a burst of energy to keep pushing forward. Other nights it'd be the b-boys 'n b-girls, spinning and popping their way across the tiles. I first learned the six step there, with my round belly hanging low, still a couple inches off the ground. Who knows? Maybe those prenatal memories are part of what has Eva Luz loving her b-girl lessons now....

Eva Luz is my first daughter. She was born April 22, 2003, to the drums and old school Palenquera singing of Petrona Martinez. Petrona, who was recording her album in the patio of the Bella Vista that night, saved me from a caesarean. Eva was busy chilling in the womb and refused to come out 'til I shook her out to the drums. Her whole first week Petrona finished up her album, and the drums were a constant. Eva Luz's first months, when she'd cry, I'd play a little drum we had at the house and she'd calm right down.

My second daughter, Maya Salome, is a month old as I write this. I shuffle between the diaper changes and the breastfeeding, I don't know what I was thinking after Eva Luz was born. I suppose it was the rush of knowing I only had two months left in Colombia, and not knowing when I'd be back. I remember feeling: she is a girl. I want her to know what she is capable of, want her to know not to sacrifice her own art. So I double-timed harder than perhaps I needed to in order to make sure I didn't sacrifice my own. When she was a week old, we held a multimedia art gig at Bella Vista. I finished and mounted my paintings, and performed a couple of songs I'd written with some cats from La HeroiK. And in those next two months, I pushed out my first homegrown demo album, featuring many of the artists I'd met. "Puntos de Luz," I called it, *Points of Light*. On the homemade covers I linoleum-printed a pregnant self-portrait. I made just enough copies to give to each of the artists who had worked with me on it, and these days can't even find my own. Not to say I'm missing much. The sound quality was terrible, and my own rhymes had a long way to go. But it was made with a hell of a lot of love. Pushing it out the hard drive of my laptop, it was like labor pains all over again.

III

Hip-Hop will make u/ struggle n claw/ will give u life real/ ready n raw...

Then we went back to Boston. With my family there to help out with the baby, I became an open mic fiend, spitting whenever I could get the chance, scribbling verses on napkins at the jazz bar where I worked nights. Freestyling to Eva as we sat around the house. At one open mic, Blackout, I met Alex King, a poet and vocalist who was also a new mother. She invited me to work with her at the Lewis Middle School in an innovative program called Our Visions Our Voices, which she had founded. Interested students had to commit to both in-school and after school hours; during these hours we would take them out of their regular classes to a black box theater in the basement. We would use Hip-Hop, art, and poetry to strengthen their regular classroom performance, talking with their teachers about their curriculum and integrating their themes into our own work. It was the most rewarding job I had had to date, watching some of the kids nobody else wanted to deal with blossom in that little room. And the best part was, I could bring the baby! Alex brought her daughter too, Journey Ade, and we'd set the two of them up in a couple of baby chairs while we worked with the students.

That was my first foray into what has become lifetime work, passing down what I know of Hip-Hop and art to the next generation, using it as a vehicle to talk with them about all the craziness they are facing and what can be done about it. After the Lewis, I worked off another grant at Fenway High School, integrating the arts into their humanities curriculum. Again, the kids took to rhymes. I did workshops at different community centers around the city. Then I was hired to start up a youth arts program to reduce youth violence by bringing together kids from across rival hoods. By then Eva Luz was two, and it was time for daycare. A woman from the neighborhood where I worked would watch her during the day, and after work we'd play for a bit in the playground before heading home for a late dinner. The schedule was hard to adjust to with her, but the work was the deepest I had done yet. Many of the relationships started while freestyling on the corner, then bit by bit the youth would come into the arts center, and together we established a workshop schedule, peer leaders, and community education sessions. We worked on Hip-Hop lyrics, dance, visual arts, percussion, and open mic sessions.

Then Dion was shot and killed. One of the first six peer leaders who'd helped me to start up the program, he'd had a keen eye for photography and a mischievous smile that made all the teenage girls go wild. And a calm, peaceful spirit that balanced out our group whenever other youth started to get heated. "I think violence really sucks," he wrote in a poem that first summer; "and I hope that someday we could officially say that there is no violence in this country or even this world ... I lost one of my best friends and others to violence that was not needed." The poem is now engraved on his gravestone, just down the cemetery from his best friend Stevie. The first time I went to visit him there, past the funeral, I remember the shock of his twin nieces, then thirteen, skipping between cemetery rows to visit the gravestones of all the other kids they knew who'd been killed. He'd been seventeen when he was killed; the kid in the grave next to his, when I did the math, had been sixteen. His nephew, Kadeem, was eight then, and sulking.

Dion had worked with us in the summer, and then decided to focus on school in the fall. But that week before he was killed in November, he'd come in to work on a portfolio of his photography and decided to stay to make a panel for a mural the rest of us were working on that day. The mural was a black and white quilt about loss, a project we were putting together for a larger exhibit called Medicine Wheel. Dion's panel had the outline of one large eye, with the pupil replaced by prison bars and a padlock. Out of the corner of the eye fell a single tear, and inside the tear he'd written FREEDOM. We found out about his death the day before the installation of the exhibit. One of the youth came knocking on my door to tell me, and I didn't believe it at first. We went to look up the news and, sure enough, there it was, in cold print. I gathered in all the youth who were out on the block, a different 'hood from his own, but he'd gained their respect and love during his work there. We sat in the dance studio on the floor and shared our memories. What it was we'd loved about him. We ate pizza. Later, a couple of the girls came with me to the Peace Institute to make pins. I don't know if other cities have the same tradition, but in Boston youth wear pins with the smiling faces of lost loved ones, rest in peace. Some kids have five, six pins on their hats, make you cringe on the subway at the smoothness of their young faces against the tragedy they carry on their heads. My boss and I called his family, invited them to an improvised memorial service at the exhibit that would open that Thursday. All week, kids flowed in and out, painting a mural of Dion, writing poetry and songs in his memory to perform at the service.

That was where I first met Stacy, his older sister who'd been like a mother to him ever since he'd come as a young kid from Trinidad to live in Boston. Because the family thought it would be safer. Stacy is an inspiration, a mother whose own home becomes a community center in a neighborhood that desperately needs one. She alone can be credited more than any grant getting non-profit for keeping those kids off the street, for helping to stop the endless cycle of revenge from one block to another. She has since become like family, Eva and Kadeem wrestling into tickling fits when they see each other. I worried sometimes about Eva back then, worried about the sadness I had her around, about the impromptu healing circles she'd have to sit in on fresh out of a day at daycare, the things she'd overhear the teenagers talking about when she sat in on rehearsals. But as she grows up, and the connections remain, I know she has had the blessings of a larger family, with all its suffering and joys, and she is definitely not a sad kid. She loves life, and knows how to play her heart out.

And there were successes, things that kept us going. There was that time at Critical Breakdown, a longstanding Boston open mic for socially conscious Hip-Hop and poetry, when some shit was about to pop off. Critical Breakdown had always been held in the 'hood, but until the arts program opened most of the wannabe thugs from the block let it alone. But now they were curious, and came in en masse, fear disguised in numbers with raucous interjections. Then one bugged out, and in a flash they were all out on the steps with another crew of kids, tossing threats. One of the youth from the program was there, one who'd done his fair share of dirt and was respected on the block. He recognized one of the kids from the other crew and calmed everyone down. Then we all went upstairs to hash it out. Turned out the other crew was a Hip-Hop dance group.

"We don't want no trouble," said one of the dancers, "That's why we started this group in the first place, after our boy Dakeem died. I lost my finger in some unnecessary bullshit like this. I'm not trying to get involved in no more beef." He showed his stunted finger. I knew Dakeem. He'd gone to the Lewis, where I'd had my first gig. He was buried in the same cemetery as Dion. Stacy had told me when we saw his grave about how she'd done daycare for his family. Sometimes, times like these, I felt their young spirits in the air.

"Why were you looking at my boy wrong then?" asked a young firestarter from the block, still trying to figure out where to put his unleashed rage.

"I was just looking. I thought I recognized him from school. I was trying to figure out if it was him or not."

"Why'd you go for your pocket like you were gonna pull out some heat?" Honestly curious now.

"Yo, man, it was just my cell phone. I was just gonna call my moms."

They all laughed, and the ice broke. Chalk one up for Hip-Hop.

Through both the losses and the successes, Eva soaked it up. Latching on to some of the teenage girls, she would beg to help add paint to a mural or sit and watch the dancers. At three she wrote her first rap verse. Open mics, she'd roll up on stage with me, back me up on hooks. Once she did her ABCs. This past summer she performed her first original poem. "Freedom is love," she told the audience, holding the mic firmer than I'd ever seen her. Evaluzion. That's the MV name she's taken. Which translates as evolution, fitting perfectly as I wonder in awe at the ways she evolves.

IV

Hip-Hop will be the language/ linking u 2 liberation/ the bridge btwn the barrios/ bringing down the corporation/ Hip-Hop will be the movement/ moving mountains in the street/ Hip-Hop will be a billion feet/ stomping out the beat…

I worked in that arts program for three years, but each year I would take some time off to come back down to Colombia with Eva Luz. We would always swing through La HeroiK, always hang with Fusion Latina, and always stay at Bella Vista. Then La HeroiK split, old school/new school. Maria Mulataz Callejeras was formed, el MMC. They'd meet three times a week too, on the patio of a DJ and *graffitero*[4] named Walter. Then we'd have two crews to visit. KP/Ruzza and Fran Zulu of Fusion Latina got married, had their first child. A girl, Zuly Gabriela, named after the Zulu Nation. Robert, one of the leaders of La HeroiK, and Eliza, one of the b-girls, also had a daughter, Natalia. Eva's generation was growing. They'd toddle or run around at Hip-Hop events, our reason to do what we do.

And then I'd come back to Boston, and the contrast with my crazy schedule would get my head spinning. I barely got to see Eva Luz, and when I did, there wasn't much space to focus on her. Her first child-care provider flopped when Eva told me she was scared of the woman's husband. I switched her to another woman from the neighborhood who'd been recommended by a friend, then when she was old enough, started her off in the bilingual preschool run by the non-profit where I worked.

I was lucky—it was on the bottom level of the arts center. But she would get done at five, and I wouldn't finish 'til six, so I would be running out in the middle of a workshop full of teenagers and their own drama to scoop her up, then have her up in the midst of it all, wanting my attention because I'd been away all day. Evenings after work I had meetings three, sometimes four days a week. Then twice a week I worked nights bartending at the jazz bar until three in the morning. All just to make ends meet—and even then they didn't always, especially in the winter months when heat bills skyrocket through the roof. Weekends, when there wasn't some performance or other associated with my work, I was often so exhausted from the rest of the week that I'd drop her by my parents' house and just rest up. I felt like I was missing out on some of her most important years. And I knew the life I wanted for her, for us, knew it was down here where the pace is built slow around the sun and there is space to spend with those you love, including yourself. Less focus on running around to make money, more willingness to do without everything that seems so necessary when I'm up in Boston, but isn't really.

This I knew ever since I'd birthed her here. But I was reluctant to raise her across the ocean from her biological father—I wanted her to have him in her life. We had tried for one disastrous year to make it work between the two of us when I'd first gotten back, but since that fell apart he'd seen her less and less. His long absences outweighed his all too occasional presence in her life, and no longer seemed like a reason to try and make it in a city whose rhythm felt so counter-intuitive to what I wanted to be as a mother.

Each time I went back and forth between Boston and Cartagena, I'd bring bits and pieces of the Hip-Hop community I was leaving behind to the community I was returning to, until little by little they began to merge into one large community that criss-crossed our continents, trying to make sense of how what happened on one side of the ocean reverberated on the other. Youth wrote letters back and forth, people sent pictures. I did workshops, translated lyrics. And out of this I sculpted my dream of the life I wanted. And so began *La Lengua de mi Barrio*, a Hip-Hop exchange program that grew from the seeds of those trips, a collective envisioning of what Hip-Hop can be capable of as a worldwide movement.

Coming back from Cartagena to Boston one year, I found one of the youth I'd worked with hard locked up for accessory to murder. We'll call him T. He was fifteen. The victim was nineteen, three weeks away from a college scholarship. His family had moved from Somalia to Boston to escape violence. Another failed image of the peaceful U.S. of A. Not on ghetto streets. His brother was the one who'd been involved in the hood-to-hood beef, but he'd been the one to take the bullet. In a crazy twist of fate, another young poet I worked with had been close to the victim. Had sat beside him on the Metco bus to school and clipped his nails. Both she and T had shared stages, had debated back and forth at workshops. Both were outspoken, and each respected the other's way with words. I am always moved by the way connections overlap. Always feel that they are a way to highlight each side's humanity when revenge is bubbling hot. But of course T never heard the poem she wrote for her lost friend, because the cops had picked him up that same night, plucking bullet shells off the crime scene.

T had written a letter after one of the workshops I'd done on Colombia's Hip-Hop movement, for me to bring down. "Yo, we banging out here in Boston too," he'd written, "but yall is on your shit. Keep it gully and bang out whatever your situation is."

Fran Zulu from Fusion Latina wrote him back:

> I believe change exists within each of us. Human beings tend to do what the majority does ... it's a question of converting ourselves into the majority, understand? If people with leadership and great intelligence, maybe like you, use it to grow this majority, everything would be different....

I brought him the letter to lockup. He read it, took it in. Young thugs in Boston seem to have a sort of awe and respect for the youth in Colombia. One too many Pablo Escobar movies, maybe. Whatever it was, Fran Zulu's words hit home with T. "I wish I'd read this earlier," he told me, his signature smirk gone. "I probably wouldn't be where I am now."

Perhaps it was his reflection that pushed me to take the next step I'd been mulling over. Perhaps it was one too many sandwiches from the corner store for my daughter's dinner, eaten on the run to yet another meeting. Maybe I was just fed up with that invisible barrier in non-profit work that lets you get just to the edge of real change and then flings you on your back because it's really in your funders' interests to keep the big picture of the status quo intact. Maybe I'd seen one too many of the real warriors around me fired. Whichever it was, or whatever combination, in 2007 I decided to take a four month leave of absence from my job in Boston. I came down here to Cartagena, Colombia. I worked on putting La Lengua onto paper, running it by everybody, determined to take it to the next level. I wanted to be able to bring youth from Boston down here, bring youth from here up there, and weave us together. I wanted our common language of Hip-Hop to help us figure out how to build the communities we deserved.

As fate would have it, I met my would-be husband, Diego, on that trip, yet another force pulling me closer to where I really wanted to be. By the end of the four months, my mind was made up. I came back to Boston to finish up my job in the best way I could, working with the youth to choose a new coordinator for the program. I gave up my lease, moved whatever furniture I had back to my family's house. I sold my car. And I moved across the ocean to build my next step in that steep, rocky, beautiful terrain that we call life.

And so it has been, little by little. In 2008, La Lengua linked up with Partners of the Americas, and hosted our first physical exchange with Lady Enchantress, a Boston artist/activist who came down here and got to know the Hip-Hop movements in both Cartagena and Medellin, then brought what she'd learned back to Boston. And helped to build the exchange up. Then brought another artist/activist, LaGuardia, down from Miami. Took him to Palenque, where he freestyled over the folkloric drums while the old men smiled into their wrinkles. In the summer of 2009, we brought two Hip-Hop artists from Colombia up to Boston, and they did workshops at many of the community centers where I'd worked, among others. The most meaningful for me was a workshop at the youth center where I'd started the arts program. Chyna Black, an amazing lyricist, artist, and poet who'd been a peer leader with me a couple years earlier, had her own after hours program going there. She introduced us to the fifteen or so youth she had gathered for their weekly lyrics workshop. A flood of happiness filled my bones seeing the woman she'd grown into, at the ripples that reverberated like the bass of a good beat. And later, as she showed me pictures of her baby son, I knew another mother would be keeping Hip-Hop alive, passing it down.

I am married, happy and in love and growing more so every day, and I have just given birth to Maya Salome, my second daughter, now a month old. I teach twelve hours a week at a university and with that I get by. I make money stretch, buy just a bag of oil for 15 cents when there's not enough for a whole bottle. I spend time with Eva Luz. We paint together, make storybooks together, freestyle together. She'll beat-box for me for a bit, and I'll rhyme, then we'll switch it up. We're both real amateur on the beat-boxing tip, but we have fun in the kitchen. And as we do, we say whatever we feel, whatever we think, which is one of the best things I have learned from Hip-Hop.

KP/Ruzza and I started El Matriarkao, our female Hip-Hop collective, with another young woman, MC Ebony. KP/Ruzza had her second baby, Zulu Samuel. Another one for the nation. He is six months old. After she gave birth she passed me her pregnancy clothes. Maya was just beginning to get round in my belly then. Now it is MC Ebony who is pregnant with her first baby. She wants to name it Africa. So I'm passing the pregnancy clothes on again. Sort of like Hip-Hop. Passed along from one heart to another to give birth to new words, new rhythms. New colors sprayed across a wall, new contortions never before known to be possible for the human body. Or from one country to another, to be reincarnated into a new language, new rhythms laid alongside the bass, new struggles bubbling under the surface, exploding into rhyme.

I am working on my first solo album. Recorded up 'til a week before Maya was born, and now taking a little break. I don't feel so rushed as I did with Eva. I know firmly that I won't be giving it up, know it's woven into the fibers of my being and my way of being a mother. I am working on my first video too. Got all my footage finished just before the birth. Gotta have that belly in the shots. Haven't touched it since, but tomorrow might just be the day to start editing. Or then again, maybe it won't be until next month. But it will be done. And in the meantime, I practice my freestyling skills while breastfeeding. I swear the rhymes calm her down. Probably all that bass she heard in the belly.

And Eva has gone b-girl. The cats I met way back in the day at La HeroiK have gotten older now. The skills passed down to them then some have decided to pass on to the next round. They've gotten permission to teach Hip-Hop workshops in a public school down the street from my house. Sunday mornings at eight a.m.! But the youth show up, eager to work. So I decided to bring Eva, who loves to dance. All that reggaeton the rest of her friends on the block drop to the ground for, well, it drives me crazy. Call me old fashioned, but I just can't stand to watch three year old girls on all fours shake-weaving their hips like whatever video girls they've been watching. So my husband and I, we tell Eva to listen to the lyrics. We talk to her about originality. We ask her to see if any of the songs pumping out the giant speakers on all the buses are saying anything new. And then we ask her about the music she hears in the house. Not just Hip-Hop. Rock, reggae, anything that's saying something new, or something that rings true to her. Her favorite song these days is "Numeros" by Los Aldaenos, a Hip-Hop group from Cuba. They wrote the song for their kids. "Esto es," goes the hook, "por si manana me voy, por si manana no estoy. Aqui te dejo mi herencia ...." Which translates into something like this: "This is in case I'm not around tomorrow, in case tomorrow I have to go... here I leave you my inheritance." In the verses they spell out everything they hope their children will learn from them. Evaluzion nods along and belts out the hook whenever the song comes on. And back from b-girl lessons, she runs to me, bright-eyed. "I have to do my break-dance homework," she tells me, and asks me to hold her feet while she practices handstands against a wall.

I can't imagine raising my daughters without Hip-Hop to help me through it. Hip-Hop the art form, its elements, gates wide open for them to explore and express, but also Hip-Hop the community, a worldwide family to help them on their paths. Hip-Hop the way of life, the questioning mind, the looking around at the world and refusing to settle for less than we deserve, the fearlessness in the face of our truth.

In my own life Hip-Hop helped me to make sense of the world at a time when it seemed most senseless—it gave me a torch to carry to light my way, and it gave me a way to walk down. It gave me a beautiful and ever-expanding community to help me along the rough spots, to cheer me on when I wanted to give up and to call me out if I started to front. And it gave me all this as I took my first tentative steps through motherhood.

In gratitude, I passed it on.

[1]Arepas are small corncakes indigenous to Colombia and Venezuela. They are spread with butter and cheese or served as a sandwich with a variety of ingredients.
[2]Spanish for neighbourhood.
[3]Sancocho is a soup traditional to many parts of Latin America. Its ingredients are often a play on the particularities of national cuisine in each region. Common features of this dish include very large chunks of vegetables and meat in a broth.
[4]Graffiti artist.

6.

Seven Generations — Mothering, Indigeneity and Hip-Hop

A Conversation with Lindsay "Eekwol" Knight

SHANA L. CALIXTE

I MOVED TO SUDBURY, ONTARIO from Toronto four years ago. As a Black queer feminist, I was worried. I didn't quite know what to expect in the mostly white, working-class city of "over 300 lakes." As a mom to a fifteen-month-old, and recently diagnosed with post-partum depression, I wasn't quite sure how I was going to survive in this city, with my community of mamas and anti-racist radicals left behind. It was almost a year later, at a session entitled, "The Politics of Hip-Hop: A Sudbury Launch Event" for the journal, *Upping the Anti*, where I started to find the community I was longing for. I presented a paper on being a Hip-Hop feminist, and the role of the music in my own experiences of community, mothering, and academia.

At this session, a fellow presenter provided a complex analysis of native Hip-Hop in Canada. It was in this presentation that I was introduced to the life saving music of artist Eekwol (Lindsay Knight). Discovering her voice, and the challenges to the Hip-Hop culture that I was already trying to complicate in my own mind, gave rise to a very fortunate "meeting" a couple of years later.

While thinking of this volume, I remembered that Eekwol had recently become a mama. I instantly knew that a talk with her about the complexities of motherhood, radical indigenous politics and Hip-Hop would benefit this collection.

I knew very little about indigenous Hip-Hop, but my sense was that the connections would be easy to make—Hip-Hop, born of struggle, becoming increasingly relevant in the politics of decolonization made it a no-brainer that folks with histories of colonization would be taking up the art form.

TRANSNATIONAL MUSICS: INDIGENOUS HIP-HOP

Most scholars note that Hip-Hop has moved beyond its roots in African-American and Latino communities in the South Bronx. In fact, the popularity of this musical form, which responds directly to marginalization and oppression, has become popular with many other groups of people who have similar, albeit different experiences of oppression.

Indigenous musical forms have included Hip-Hop beats for some time now, and many groups, many from Canada, have just started to break into mainstream music with their contributions to the Hip-Hop music industry.[1] Overlooked for many years due to assumptions about what kinds of music Indigenous groups produced,[2] many acts have been breaking into the scene, gathering awards and gaining a considerable following.

Scholars investigating the production of "indigenous Hip-Hop" have discussed the use of Hip-Hop as a transnational as well as anti-colonial practice.[3] The global literacy of Hip-Hop has manifested in the production of Hip-Hop on many other continents, like Europe and Asia, and in other places where struggle is a dominant theme. As Greg Dimitriadis writes in *Performing Identity/Performing Culture,*

> The uptake of hip hop around the world is intriguing—marked, as it has been by an assertion of the local. That is, as hip hop has circulated around the world, it has become a vehicle for the disenfranchised youth to articulate their own local needs and concerns. (xiv)

This theme has been evidenced in many other spaces, including the very interesting anti-occupation film, *Slingshot Hip Hop*, about the music culture in Palestine. Various "displaced tribes" have found a space within Hip-Hop to speak truth to power, to "learn how to position themselves, as well as contest how they have been positioned, within struggles over power" (Lashua 4).

Hip-Hop, developed and sustained by indigenous communities, has a complex history in Canada. A quick look at the various forms the music has taken over the past 20 years unveils a mix of radical political lyrics, local musical traditions and a strong identification with the experiences of African-American artists.[4] As Sarah Efron notes,

89

SHANA L. CALIXTE

> Hip-Hop has overtaken both heavy rock and traditional pow-
> wow music as the music of choice on the reserves, and Native
> MCs, DJs, graffiti artists, and break-dancers are popping up
> everywhere. It's not surprising, considering that 56 percent of
> Canada's aboriginal population is less than 24 years old. Many
> grow up in poverty and identify with the rap lyrics from the
> African-American ghettos.

In Efron's interview with Manik, an MC and member of the Vancouver based collective *Tribal Wizdom*,[5] this artist discusses how using Hip-Hop to target and examine the experiences of Indigenous populations in the country is vital: "I have to help my people feel better any way I possibly can, and it just so happens that I can rap. The Creator gave me my words to say to my people at this vital time when there is this hip-hop revolution going on" (Efron). Some have noted a concern from elders about the new focus on this "revolution" and the worries about the loss of "traditional" musical genres and a mainstreaming of aboriginal musical culture (Alteen).[6] Those heavily involved in the scene argue that this is not a movement away from the "old" and offer up a (re) embracing of the "traditional" (however we understand that, in all of its complexity) with a contemporary twist. Spoken word, dance, oral histories—these are all a perfect landscape to craft an indigenous Hip-Hop "tradition." Alteen states:

> Aboriginal artists have taken hip hop influences and indigenized
> them to fit Aboriginal experiences: The roots of hip hop are
> there but they have been ghost-danced by young Native artists
> who use hip hop culture's artistic forms and combine them with
> Aboriginal story, experience and aesthetics. (Willard)

Hip-Hop has become a tool for activism. *Beat Nation* provides a look at how artists have indigenized many Hip-Hop cultural practices, from graffiti to break dancing to fashion to media, and of course the music itself. Hip-Hop has become a tool to reignite a project of decolonization within the most marginalized ranks of First Nations communities: the young.

As scholars note, youth have taken up Hip-Hop quite deliberately, as a way to de-center the dominant whiteness in mainstream music, and to reactively effect change within grassroots organizing. In the early 1990s, youth within the Cree nation in Western Canada (most specifically in Alberta) had begun creating a strong Hip-Hop music culture, albeit quite underground and non-commercialized (Krims 2000). In his discussion with Cree MC Bannock, Adam Krim details the very "local and global" flow of the music created by many Cree youth in Edmonton, which is used to underscore the flexibility of an identity he calls "Creeness" and to speak back to the representation of young aboriginal people as simply gangsters and layabouts.[7] This is happening across Canada.

In Winnipeg in 2009, StreetzFM 104.7 was launched. Aimed at the young Aboriginal community who enjoy and identify with Hip-Hop, the station is targeting an audience that continues to be marginalized in Manitoba's largest city. Identifying Hip-Hop as a main way of attracting this community of youth speaks to the usefulness of linking music with struggle. Something that Hip-Hop has done for many a community, and something that has been "a way to attract both urban and rural Native youth to become more aware of our rights, histories and cultures" (Alteen). The indigenizing of Hip-Hop spans not only territories and nations, but also ethnic/cultural groups within Turtle Island's indigenous communities as well as the urban/rural divide. It truly is, as Manik stated, a "hip hop revolution." What has also been evidenced in Canada has been a bridging of struggle between Black and indigenous communities through the use of Hip-Hop. In 2007, Six Nations MC Shiloh spoke on Toronto radio to discuss the work that could be done through Black and indigenous solidarity. This link speaks to the voluminous ways that Hip-Hop can not only work to build bridges, but to think of ways to connect the struggles of colonized peoples who exist on the same land.

But what about women? It seems to be the ongoing chorus when talking about any musical genre, and it is not surprising that the voices of women are also marginalized in the growing community of indigenous Hip-Hop music creators. There are a few who have broken into the musical scene, including Calgary-born Mohawk artist Kinnie Star and Cree artist Eloquence. However, one of the larger names out there is Eekwol, whose contribution to Indigenous music has shed light on the important feminist aspects that the music can make to the project of decolonization and to the topic at hand, radical motherhood.

ABOUT EEKWOL

Eekwol has been dubbed Saskatoon's "first lady of hip hop" and her presence as a female emcee is not to be ignored (Siliphant 2009: 31). Her lyrical style has been described as "charismatic" and "smooth" with "a balanced and healthy taste of experimental hip hop that comes from her land and place while respecting the history and place of original hip hop."[8] Originally from Saskatchewan and the Muskoday First nation, Eekwol has been working on her music, with her brother Mils since they were kids:

> Because [Mils and I] grew up together and are so close in age. We started with making forts and playing marbles, [moving on] to shooting cheap skate or horror vids, to air banding to Dad's records with an audience of stuffed animals and G.I. Joes. So as you can see, it's a seamless transition into making hip-hop music (Siliphant 2007).

And seamless it has been. Breaking onto the scene in 1998, she has released eight albums and has been featured on several other discs, as well as in both film and television. Her music has been recognized nationally and internationally, garnering her the First Nations Arts and Entertainment Award in 2008 and the Best Rap/Hip-Hop album of the year at the Canadian Aboriginal Music Awards in 2005. Working with her brother, she created Mils Productions, an independent production company, where she has collaborated with Stic.Man of DeadPrez and many others in both Japan and Australia.

Eekwol is clear about her lyrical focus: "We must question everything if we ever want to get anywhere" (Nativehiphop.net). She has done so on the many albums she has recorded and produced, but also in the work she has taken up, through education and activism, focusing on decolonization. Her music reflects her Plains Cree background, outlining the impact that indigenizing Hip-Hop can have on the music and culture.

> I also use a lot of Cree language, in an attempt to retain the knowledge and teachings that come with the Plains Cree worldview, in a very cool, non-cheesy, new school hip hop sort of way. Let's just say, I know how to freak it so that the hip hop

heads, gangsters, nerds, warriors, babies and Elders can feel and get something out of listening to my music. (Siliphant 2009: 31)

Eekwol's most recent album, *Niso* (2010), means "two" in Cree and, as she says, "signifies my two cultural backgrounds, and how everything is divided, and it becomes a continuous struggle to balance my identity" (Siliphant 2009: 31). Eekwol took a little break since the birth of her son, Keesik in 2008, but also sees the importance of "two" with regards to mothering. "I now think and act for two ... and that means feeding him the right knowledge in hopes that he will be a compassionate, aware and conscious human being" (Silliphant 2009: 31).

In this interview with Eekwol, I wanted to know three things: A bit about her life, a bit more about her music and quite a bit about her thoughts on the intersections of mothering and Hip-Hop. While her two-year-old son napped, and my four-year-old meandered around the house with his other mom, we had a quick online conversation about these three things and the way music has come to represent, for her, a continued engagement with decolonization and "seven generation sustainability" (Siliphant 2009: 31).

FUTURE WONDERS[9]: A CONVERSATION WITH EEKWOL

Shana Calixte (SC): Okay, so can you tell me a bit about your growing up? Your childhood?

Lindsay "Eekwol" Knight (LEK): I grew up mostly in Saskatoon, and spent some time on our reserve, Muskoday, because all of our family was there. We were pretty poor and made do with what we had and I'm grateful for that today because it shaped my understanding and that comes out in my lyrics. I grew up as a half-breed, so that had its challenges. Overall, it was all right as far as that goes, however, I only understood the Plains Cree way of doing things because my mom (Russian) had sort of been disowned for marrying an Indian. This was the late '70s so it was REALLY unacceptable at that time ... nobody worried about being PC at that time.

SC: Speaking of lyrics, how were you introduced to Hip-Hop?

LEK: As an "urban Indian" we were exposed to Hip-Hop through movies like *Boys N the Hood*, unfortunately! We saw much of the negative styles of rap and I was in love with Tupac since I was about 13 years old

... I loved how he was able to put stories to a beat, making it simple and relatable, yet with deep meaning. There were many similarities in our area to do with violence, addictions and street life, so it was a compatible way of expression because we really have been so stripped of our own cultural ways and identity for so many years ... as young people, you turn somewhere whether it's positive or negative.

SC: I did love me some *Boyz N the Hood*, I get that.

LEK: It wasn't long before I was introduced to underground Hip-Hop and that was sort of earth shattering for me because here were rappers rapping about social change and pertinent issues ... that was kinda my thing in my late teenage years, so that's how I really took off full force as a lyricist and performer.

SC: I really hear you about the way that Hip-Hop can speak the stories of so many people. How have people thought about indigeneity and Hip-Hop? Can you speak more to that and how the music provides a space for community? Or how you feel you've used the music in this way?

LEK: Totally, as our Indigenous cultures have always been narrative and oral history the foremost way of transmitting memory, it's almost a seamless transition into Hip-Hop/spoken word ... it's no wonder why it's so popular in Indian country, because it's storytelling that crosses from urban to rural and connects traditional to contemporary. In fact, many indigenous (and probably other cultures) rappers have begun using traditional instrumentation and language within their Hip-Hop, including myself as I have begun rapping in Cree. It feels good to incorporate these things.

SC: This is so powerful. For me, I think there needs to be more discussions about how communities with histories of colonization can see how music can provide this connection. There is always this talk about "appropriation" without political analysis, so this is really significant to hear.

LEK: (laughing out loud) I'm actually doing my Masters thesis on this topic, in a way!

SC: Oh really! That is so so great! I did a bit of looking to see what I should read in this area and can see there is a growing body of work. I definitely want to read your thesis!

LEK: Music and songs were once more than entertainment, they were a part of our governance and societal, spiritual and economic structure as there were songs for EVERYTHING ... this is what I'm trying to bring back in order to regain pride in our cultures as indigenous ... .the genres

94

of music are not what needs to be focused on, it's how we are respectfully Indigenizing, is that a word? (laughing), these options to strengthen our lost communities.

SC: So does motherhood fall into this in any way? How has it been to see your music as a mom to a little one?

LEK: World changing ... I had always boasted the importance of thinking and acting for the next seven generations, but now I really get it! My life, including lyrics have changed significantly since Keesik was born. I released an album for him titled, *Niso*, where I have a song dedicated to his perfection at the same time another song about how difficult it was becoming a new mother as I suffered PPD. I'm even more honest than I was previously because I feel we don't have much time to beat around the bush these days as the colonization continues.

SC: I also had PPD (have?) ... ahhh motherhood, what folks don't tell you about it ...

LEK: No doubt! It was pretty scary ... I had never suffered depression and now I know what that's all about and I really feel for peeps who live that way ... anyway

SC: One sec! I am on potty break duty. Be right back.

* * *

SC: Back. He says "hi". So when thinking about Hip-Hop, what challenges do you think motherhood presents to the genre?

LEK: I guess the obvious is the gender issue as it is predominantly male and very male oriented ... I've always struggled with that before I was a mom, and now I thought I'd be more ostracized than ever, and guess what? I am in the sense that the purist Hip-Hop community has sort of left me alone, yet a whole other way cooler, intelligent and more progressive audience has taken its place, so I'm happy to share the Hip-Hop that I know and understand to a wider audience such as indigenous communities, academic community, and indie/emo kids ... very cool indeed. I was growing very tired of the way the Hip-Hop community in my area was becoming ... or not becoming, maybe just staying the same, so I'm not really too involved ... plus, I can't really do many late nights anymore so that may be something to do with it!

SC: Ha! Indeed. Why do you think the "purists" have left you alone? Is the space for motherhood in Hip-Hop contentious?

LEK: An example of this transition is the main DJ who used to hire me to open for all the big acts rolling through Saskatoon has stopped calling me ... not too long ago his facebook status said, "Make moves, not babies" so there ya go.

SC: WOW. I don't know why I'm saying wow. I guess this shouldn't surprise me, but what what? AS IF.

LEK: Yea, because he's not being very PC? He's just stating what runs through many male minds, I think. Once they have babies, they're off the market so to speak! That sounds a little extreme, but I think it holds some truth around here.

SC: You work with your brother right? How is that and has he commented on the change in your music and the reaction of some of the community?

LEK: Oh, my brother is cool with it because he has two little ones! In fact, our reality is that we have very little to no time to work on music anymore because of our family duties ... he lives a ways away so we don't see each other to often anymore ... maybe when the kiddies are older.

SC: Ah yeah ... so many changes in life when the babies are around.... So in the day to day, how is Keesik involved in your music? I saw a great pic of you performing and him hanging out in the grass.

LEK: He's always coming with me to every event because my husband is very hands on and a great dad. We've traveled quite a bit as a family unit and it works really well. I'm pretty blessed. Keesik's been on stage with me a few times, no fear whatsoever. He kinda dances and raps on the mic ... baby talk style! He has a tendency to steal my show! I love having him around as a new dynamic.

SC: What do you want him to know about music, Hip-Hop, as he gets older?

LEK: For me, motherhood and my music are very comfortable. I'm so happy. I really don't care about what others think and feel as they aren't good for business to begin with. It's a relief to feel so clear about my direction with music because of being a mom. You know what it's like when you no longer have time for bullshit ... I get snappy at cashiers when I used to just patiently wait or let things slide. I'm just way more assertive in all aspects of life. I want Kee to understand the origins of Hip-Hop and his Cree roots as they both shape who his mommy is. He can make his decisions from there. He's very musical already, so I know he'll be involved in some way ... it's exciting to see!

SC: You did talk about that earlier—about not having time to sit around cuz colonialism is still going—how do you see Hip-Hop addressing this?

LEK: Very effectively ... we have quite a few indigenous rappers discussing decolonization and revolution, gaining momentum through groups like the Native Youth Movement. It's an attractive space for open dialogue about our original history and what needs to happen in order for our people to get free and healthy ... many young people are becoming more aware and it's awesome to see ... as I said, young Indian country loves Hip-Hop, so why not use it as a means to decolonize? As for motherhood, I'm raising a warrior by teaching him all that I know about love and kindness, our history and how beautiful our music, culture, traditions and people are ... this is my most important job, to give him these tools to use as he sees fit. I hope that he'll be strong to fight the battle that we've been fighting for 500+ years. I love the feeling that Hip-Hop gives me ... it's so rich with creativity and stems from a place of struggle and emancipation ... it's the same feeling I get when I'm with Keesik ... it can only be understood by another mother ... just a damn good feeling that everything is alright in the universe, even if it's just for that moment!

SC: And I'm sure most folks want to know—how did you come up with your chosen name, Eekwol?

LEK: Eekwol is actually Lowkee backwards as that's the name I started out with back in '95 (when Hip-Hop was real ... LOL, just kidding!) ... but I switched it because there were many Lowkeys popping up so I wanted something original ... plus it sounds like equality, what I'm always working towards ... not sameness, but equal-ness!

SC: I love that. And yes, Hip-Hop was HOTTT back in the '90s. I do agree.

LEK: You know it lady!

SC: Thank you so much Lindsay. This has been great.

LEK: Just in time ... Keesik's awake!

[1]Some acts have been highlighted at various mainstream music award shows, like the Junos. Team Rezoffiical was the first indigenous Hip-Hop group to make it to the number one spot on MuchMusic's *Rap City* countdown in 2008—five years after the group came together (see Morris). Independent festivals, like the First Nations Hip-Hop festival, started in 2004 in Saskatchewan, continue to highlight up and coming acts.
[2]As Ullestead notes, there are "two distinct poles of artistic expression (assumed about Indigenous peoples' music): traditionalist and commercial/assimilationist" (64).

3I have chosen to use the words "indigenous" and "indigenous peoples" rather than "native," "first nations" or "aboriginal" quite deliberately. Although "indigenous' signals many people around the world, and my focus here is only on "Canadian" artists, I use this politicized term to make a link to all those who live in occupied lands and who identify with a radical politics of decolonization. As Linda Tuhiwai Smith notes, "the term has enabled the collective voices of colonized people to be expressed strategically in the international arena" (7). I do note, however, that by using this naming I have essentially spoken for many groups who have named the cultural production in other ways. For more on the term "indigenous" and the importance of naming and language when speaking about communities under occupation, see Tuhiwai Smith.

4This paper cannot fully document the number of Hip-Hop groups and collectives within indigenous communities. For a fuller list of artists and work, see http://www.nativehiphop.net/. Artists of note include Team Rezofficial, Tru Rez, Kinnie Star, and War Party (now defunct). Also, the wide variety of indigenous Hip-Hop around the world should also be investigated (specifically work in Australia and the U.S.) as it provides an important context to the development of Hip-Hop in Canada.

5Shawn Desjarlais started the Tribal Wizdom collective, bringing together MCs who would focus on the important concerns of youth, effect change through decolonization using the tools of Hip-Hop (rapping, break dancing, graffiti and DJing). It is also a part of the Native Youth Movement, a non-profit organization aimed at youth with a similar mandate, bridging indigenous youth collectives across Canada and the U.S. (Desjarlais).

6Glenn Alteen is one of the producers of the online showcase of indigenous cultural production, *Beat Nation: Hip Hop as Indigenous Culture.* <http://www.beatnation.org/index.html>.

7<http://www.beatnation.org/index.html>.

8Eekwol. Myspace page. <http://www.myspace.com/eekwol/>.

9This is the title of a song on Eekwol's 2004 album, *Apprentice to the Mystery.*

WORKS CITED

Alteen, Glenn. *Beat Nation: Hip Hop as Indigenous Culture.* Web. <http://www.beatnation.org/index.html>.

Amadahy, Zainab and Bonita Lawrence. "Indigenous Peoples and Black

People in Canada: Settlers or Allies?" *Breaching the Colonial Contract: Anti-Colonialism in the U.S. and Canada*. Ed. Arlo Kempf. Dordrecht: Springer, 2009. 105-132.

Desjarlais, Shawn. "Rediscovering Tribal Wizdom." *Wiretap; Alternet*, 2003. Web. <http://www.alternet.org/wiretap/15530/?page=1>.

Dimitriadis, Greg. *Performing Identity/Performing Culture: Hip-hop as Text, Pedagogy, and Lived Practice*. New York: Peter Lang, 2009.

Efron, Sarah. "Native Hip-Hoppers Rap Out Their Message." *The Georgia Straight*, 2001. Web. <www.sarahefron.com/stories/tribal-wizdom.shtml>.

Featured Artists: Eekwol. Nativehiphop.net, 2009. Web. <http://www.nativehiphop.net/featured-artists/eekwol/

Hollands, Robert. "Rappin' on the Reservation: Canadian Mohawk Youth's Hybrid Cultural Identities." *Sociological Research Online* 9.3 (2004). Web. <http://www.socresonline.org.uk/9/3/hollands.html>.

Krims, Adam. *Rap Music and the Poetics of Identity: New Perspectives in Music History and Criticism*. Cambridge: Cambridge University Press, 2000.

Lakhani, Ali, Vanessa Oliver, Jessica Yee, Randy Jackson and Sarah Flicker. "Keep the Fire Burning Brightly: Aboriginal Youth Using Hip Hop to Decolonize a Chilly Climate." *Climate Change: Who's Carrying the Burden? The Chilly Climates of the Global Environmental Dilemma*. Eds. L. Anders Sandberg and Tor Sandberg. Ottawa: Canadian Centre for Policy Alternatives, 2010. 205-212.

Lashua, Brett David. *Making Music, Re-making Leisure in The Beat of Boyle Street*. Unpublished Dissertation, University of Alberta. Edmonton, Alberta, 2005.

Mitchell, Tony. *Global Noise: Rap and Hip-Hop Outside the USA*. Middletown: Wesleyan University Press, 2001.

Morris, Chereise. "Rezofficial Hit Number One on MuchMusic Rap City." *Alberta Sweetgrass: The Aboriginal newspaper of Alberta* 15.10 (2008): 1.

Native Tongues, Hip Hop's Global Indigenous Movement: A roundtable curated by Christina Véran, with Daryl "DLT" Thompson, Litefoot, Grant Leigh Saunders, Mohammed Yunus Rafiq and JASS. *Total Chaos: The Art and Aesthetics of Hip-Hop*. Ed. Jeff Change. New York: Basic Civitas, 2006. 278-292.

Sakolsky, Ron. "Boyz From the Rez: An Interview with Robby Bee."

Sounding Off! Music as Subversion/Resistance/Revolution. Eds. Ron Sakolsky and Fred Wei-han Ho. New York: Autonomedia, 1995. 163-170.

"Say Ambassadors." *Say Magazine*, 2006. Web. <http://www.saymag.com/canada/spokespeople.php>.

Sealy, David. "Eekwol Opportunity." *Degrees Magazine*, Fall 2007. Regina: University of Regina. Web. <http://www.uregina.ca/news/degrees.php?issue=3&article=6>.

Siliphant, Craig. "Hip-Hop 2.0: Lyrical Maturity, Masterful Production Mark Dynamic Duo's Latest." *Planet S Magazine* October 11, 2007.

Siliphant, Craig. "Baby on Board." *Planet S Magazine* 9.1 (2009): 31.

Slingshot Hip Hop. DVD. Directed by Jackie Salloum. 2008.

Tuhiwai Smith, Linda. *Decolonizing Methodologies.* London: Zed Books, 2002.

Willard, Tania. "Medicine Beats and Ancestral Rhymes." *Beat Nation: Hip Hop as Indigenous Culture*, 2009. Web. <http://www.beatnation.org/index.html>.

Windspeaker Staff. "Eekwol (Lindsay Knight) — [windspeaker confidential]" *Windspeaker* 28.6 (2010). Web. <http://www.ammsa.com/publications/windspeaker/eekwol-lindsay-knight-%E2%80%94-windspeaker-confidential>.

7.

"Mommy, I'm in Anomolies too!"

A Conversation Between Two Members of an All-Female Hip-Hop Collective

SHANTELENA MOUZON (HELIXX C. ARMAGEDDON) WITH SHARON MILLER (PRI THE HONEYDARK)

BEING A MOTHER IS HARD. Being a mother in Hip-Hop is even harder and there is no training manual. You earn your stripes along the way. Not only are we committed to the well being of our children, we are also committed to the nurturing of our art form. Sometimes the two clash and begin to compete with one another. And this is where the challenge begins. My name is Helixx C. Armageddon. I am a lyricist from Queens, New York. In 1995, I co-founded the Anomolies, an all-female Hip-Hop collective. Anomolies was built on the idea that women needed a strong support system to survive in the Hip-Hop industry. It was this particular support system that led Pri the Honeydark, a well-noted MC and music producer, who was also from Queens, New York, to join the Anomolies. She is currently the founder of The Female Producers Association, which is a networking organization for creative women across the globe. When Pri joined the Anomolies, she was the only member with a child. Her son Harlon, nicknamed Groovie, was four years old at that time. Pri the Honeydark and I decided to sit down and discuss the challenges of raising our sons within Hip-Hop culture. The following is the conversation that ensued.

HIP-HOP MOTHERS

Helixx: My son Nasir was born in the year 2000. At the time of his birth, I was lucky to have you as a friend and as a part of my musical family. Having you around allowed me the benefit of learning from your challenges and experiences as a mother. You paved the way for me as a parent and made everything a lot easier. I think back to when I first met you and Harlon. You were in school full-time, you had a full-time job, you were in a music group with your son's father, called *Afrobluu,* and you were committed to helping your son work through his autism. I can only imagine what your experiences were like. Before we start talking about what being a mother in Hip-Hop means, let's start with talking about what it's like to be a mother in general. Prior to you expressing yourself creatively, how did you manage being a mom?

Pri: Well I can tell you right now it wasn't easy (sighs). Raising a child with autism is one of the hardest challenges you can face. You can't communicate with your child like you see other moms doing. I used to sit in the playground and watch other mothers speak with their two year olds and four year olds. I always wondered what that was like. My son spoke to me in occasional one-word statements and moans. Most of the time he cried in frustration. He didn't start talking in complete sentences until age seven. It was a very emotional period for all of us, including his dad. I remember being so broke that I would skip meals in order for him to eat. I was STARVING! I also remember going to school full-time and working full-time. As you know, I studied psychology because I thought I would have a better understanding of how my son's mind worked. I also was an artist, so I began teaching him how to draw and teaching him the concept of all art being created with "lines, letters and numbers." This concept was a little trick I taught him on how to simplify complicated artwork and paintings. His father and I were both creatively inclined. His father was a graffiti artist and Hip-Hop DJ and I was an interior designer and Hip-Hop lyricist. My son was born into Hip-Hop (laughs). We were a very creative family. That creativity along with our love for music and art helped to shape Harlon and also helped him to overcome his autism. Now you would never know his autism even existed in the first place.

Helixx: I totally agree. I also remember coming to your house and seeing a huge freshly painted graffiti piece on your living room wall (laughs), with turntables set-up in front of it. I knew we would be friends for a long time after I saw that.

Pri: Remember that? (Laughter) I remember when my grandmother came to my house and began screaming, "SHARON!"... Ooops ... just exposed my "government" name. She was like, "Sharon! Call the cops! Someone has broke in and vandalized your apartment!" I was like ... No Nana! We did that. It's just an art piece. She was like, "You mean, your house is supposed to look like that?" (Laughs) I said Yes Nana it's Hip-Hop.

Helixx: Being a mom has been an interesting experience for me. I knew that it wasn't a cakewalk, but somehow I never realized how overwhelming parenting could be. Like you, I was a fairly young mother. I had Nasir when I was 21 years old. At 21, I was living the life of your a-typical independent musician. I was living on my own, putting out records, doing shows, attending networking events, anticipating new collaborations, traveling and constantly trying to push my art and myself to its limits. When I found out I was pregnant, I immediately had to make adjustments in my life. I couldn't attend shows because now the environment wasn't necessarily conducive to the fragile life I was nurturing inside of me. Between smoke filled venues and testosterone infused events where fights were always possible, I had to pick and choose what I could attend and what I couldn't. Also, the further along I progressed through pregnancy, the harder it was to travel. For instance, I did a track for a production team that was signed to a major label in Japan. The record release for their project was in France. They asked me if I could perform at the release as I was just entering my eighth month of pregnancy. I went to my doctor and asked his opinion on whether or not I should fly out for the event. My doctor told me there were no guarantees Nasir would wait until I got back to NYC to arrive; my doctor jokingly said he would not be sitting on a ten or more hour flight to come to Paris to deliver him. I asked Invincible, another Anomolies member, to go to Paris in my place and perform my song. She was able to oblige and it all worked out of course. That's just one example of how I had to adjust my routines and environment to prepare for my unborn son. While I was pregnant I got signed, which allowed me to stay home with Nasir leading up to his birth. I was at home for the first year of his life, but that presented a whole other set of challenges. Now my art was paying for health care and the food on the table, so I really needed to hustle to make the big dream happen. Health care was something I couldn't be negligent in at all. Nasir has asthma, sensitive skin and is allergic to many things. His health care regimen requires any adult with him to carry an EpiPen in the event an anaphylactic reaction occurs. This had me frantic on the road. I constantly felt guilty anytime I had to do a show out of state. The maternal connection is strong and biological. It made leaving him for too long very hard. I would miss him terribly during travel, but shows are a reality for every musician and paid shows are a necessity for anyone trying to live off of their art.

Pri: I can relate to that! Do you feel that being away from Nasir, or as we like to call him, Nazzy, had any input on the relationship you and him have now?

Helixx: I think it has made a great impact on the relationship I have with him now. He is a very wise young man who shows an incredible amount of resilience at a young age. Resilience is a learned attribute that I'm sure he built up over time from not having his parents around as much as he'd like. His father and I ended our relationship when Nasir was three years old. I am his primary caretaker and the head of my household. I work very hard to spend quality time with him whenever I can and the love between us shows. His dad, my family, his community, my support network and I are raising Nasir. I could never have done it alone. How did Groovie deal with you being away before he was old enough to travel with us for shows?

Pri: Truthfully, I don't think he really understood when he was younger. Mainly because, I always showed up (laughs), so he did not have any sense of abandonment. As he became older however, he did not like the fact of me going away. I believe that was because, A: he was used to being around me 24-7 and B: He had begun his own "Hip-Hop journey" and wanted to experience what I experienced. When I speak to him now about it, he states that it never really bothered him, because he knew I would be back.

Helixx: I really think the cool thing about it is now Groovie gets to travel with us for shows and see you in action. Not only does he know you're coming back; he knows you are doing something you love to do and that's perform. He has been to quite a few shows with us now and has seen some of the good, the bad and the ugly associated with this industry. How do you deal with the imagery and adult themes that are often associated with the Hip-Hop industry?

Pri: Well … first off I explained to him the difference between Hip-Hop and the rap industry as we know it. Based on those explanations, he understands Hip-Hop is a culture. It is something we live. We live this culture whether we put out a record, make a music video or enter into television dance shows etc. You see we will always be MCs. We will always be B-girls. We will always be Graff artists & DJs. The rap industry is just that, an "industry." It deals with the commercial product and sales of goods. The industry does not care about the culture, which is why the adult themes tend to exist today in the first place. I made sure to teach my son early on the value of a woman. I also taught him early on about the influence of the rap industry and how the images are not there to view as truths. To this day, he is against the way music is presented currently and how women are projected. He seems to have a clear understanding of how to separate reality from propaganda.

Helixx: Yeah, I totally agree. I would also add the propaganda starts earlier and earlier, especially for African-American children. I struggle with media, because the stereotypes reinforce negative role models for minorities no matter where you look. Rappers reinforce these themes in music videos and songs while helping the media machine create an oppressed outlook for our youth. I work tirelessly to provide Nasir with context to songs. I'm always sourcing for Hip-Hop artists that provide a healthy alternative to the music that demoralizes our culture. I really enjoyed the 90s music scene for this very reason. Hip-Hop was diverse. You had balance. There was no one record label formula to a hit record. No single sound.

Pri: I so agree. Since there was such a diverse mixture of Hip-Hop artists, you had more of an opportunity to expose your son to a variety of styles. You had a better way of proving your point then. Now since there seems to be a "one sound" industry, it makes it slightly difficult to break down the culture of Hip-Hop, when you have nothing to compare it to.

Helixx: Exactly! You had artists like Organized Konfusion, Tupac, N.W.A., Eric B. and Rakim, M.C. Lyte, Public Enemy and many others that allowed an aficionado to hear the world through many different perspectives. Now the only perspective is the one the industry has decided is best suited to get major airplay. This poses a huge challenge for parents of young music connoisseurs especially African-American boys. They are force-fed images of Black men in jail and as criminals every day, with only music or sports as a recipe for success or the idea of engaging in illegal activity. It feels like brainwashing after a while. I feel like I am fighting against society on behalf of my son many days. What do you think?

Pri: I expose my son to a lot of diversity within Hip-Hop music with the understanding that he is well aware of the differences. He listens to everything from The Cold Crush Brothers, Common Sense and Run DMC, to Public Enemy, Wu-tang, J Dilla & M.O.P. I feel as long as your child is taught early on about right from wrong and the power of influence, the negative images presented to him or her will be just that negative. The child will not emulate what he or she feels to be harmful. This is my belief.

Helixx: Also, years ago you saw many different types of female artists. Now video vixens have replaced female artists. This is yet another image that is not balanced and very different from my experience growing up through Hip-Hop. I think providing Nasir with all the musical elements that mimic real life is key to giving him a realistic view of everything Hip-Hop has to offer.

Pri: Yeah, unfortunately right now Hip-Hop is one big music video. The MC art form itself is not lost in our culture, but seems to have lost its importance in the industry, as we know it now. I am not a video vixen! I am not a troll either! (Laughs). I am a hard working mother who can rhyme her behind off and who loves the culture I am in! How do you think our kids view us as MCs in this industry? Does Nazzy ever talk to you about it?

Helixx: I think that our children are honorary members of Anomolies! (Laughs) They sit through the creative process watching us write the music, record the music, practice the music, then they come with us to shows. They get to see confident women in a male dominated industry full cycle and the great part is we just so happen to be their mothers. Our children have an inside view of the daily struggle we go through to pursue our dreams. This first hand knowledge creates a real world scenario of how a person can carve out a creative space for him or herself in this world without compromising what they believe in. Pri, we've heard and seen many African-American males opting out of getting jobs or an education to pursue hip hop careers. What advice do you give Harlon on how to navigate life's waters when pursuing art, especially since he is now 18 and seeking a career in animation? How have you used your experiences in Hip-Hop to advise him on his career goals?

Pri: Well since Harlon was already around us during the performances, the traveling, the studio sessions, the networking, etc., he already has a sense of how things need to be in order to get things done. I also make sure he understands that in any career there are gazillions of mini careers. For example, if he wanted to pursue a career as a recording artist, I would make sure he was also aware of all of his options. Although he can be an artist, he can also be a music producer, entertainment lawyer or owner of a label using his creativity to put out others just like him. As you know, he is an illustrator and his goal is to be an animator. He realizes that he can illustrate for a company, become an animation colorist, become a storyboard artist or even start his very own independent animation studio. He has chosen the latter. I am not trying to deter my son from his goals, just making sure he is aware of everything he may be interested in and is capable of. I feel that a lot of times, kids view hip hop careers with blinders on. They don't see the other opportunities or possibilities. They just know what they see in videos. This industry is not about making a record, putting out a music video and reaping millions! It's about so much more. What about the writing, the branding, the accounting, the marketing, the promoting, the shows, the networking, the contracts, the ownership of you and your name by a label, the lack of money during your first few years? After all, this is a business and with any business you need a start-up period. Sometimes that can take years. In the meantime, what do you do? How do you support you and your family? How do you pay for health care? Kats are just leaving their jobs out of a want, but without any clear path on how to get there. There seems to be 9 million rappers on Facebook and 8.9 million of them are probably standing on the unemployment line! I tell my son don't be stupid! Keep your day job and work on your main goal every other given minute! You will be able to support yourself until you begin to reap the benefits of your career endeavors and it will definitely be worth it. I will always support my son in everything he does … as long as it's legal (laughs). I believe in his talents. What about you Helixx? I am throwing you the same question.

Helixx: Well, I consistently provide Nasir with experiential learning. I think it's important to instill a good value system in the young and build up their self-esteem. It's hard out there and a child's self esteem should always be handled with care. I remember when I was growing up; most of the African-American boys in my neighborhood were either dead or in jail before they turned 21. Very few made it out of the neighborhood alive and with a clean record. Those that survived through the formative years were considered exceptions, not necessarily the norm. My parents started exposing me and my brother to experiences outside of the neighborhood, which allowed us to see more of what life had to offer. I try to expose Nasir to all different types of learning opportunities and experiences so that he will experience life for all that it has to offer. I remember speaking to a male friend many years ago about where we both saw ourselves in 10 years. I remember distinctly he saw himself living and dying in the 'hood and never venturing outside of it. When my son was born, I promised myself I would travel with him and allow him to sample everything that awaited him outside of the door. I didn't want him to see limits to who or what he could be. Right now, my son has an interest in technology. Should he wake up tomorrow and say he wants to pursue a music career, I will support him wholeheartedly. Since birth, through his environment, he has been unconsciously gathering the tools and understanding that would allow for him to be successful in whatever path he chooses.

Pri: Hmmm ... being a mother is deep! (Laughs) I know Nazzy sees you as a role model, but how hard do you think it is to be a positive role model to Nasir when young boys are traditionally taught to emulate men not women?

Helixx: It's been challenging for me. I just try to do my best to display the universal qualities I hope will rub off on him. I am not a man and I don't claim to understand all things male. I always try to be there for him and am very honest with him about my knowledge-base. I always let him know if I can't answer a question he has, we can dig into our pool of resources to get the answer. I not only try to lead by example, but I put him around males that lead by example too. I try to show him that life is a spectrum. Nothing in life is absolute. I know that he may try to glean from his male peers the answers to questions he may think I won't understand. I can sympathize with him. I would much rather have a female peer tell me about a menstrual cycle than a male peer unless he is a doctor, so I get that there are certain instances where a specific gender may be a preferred source of information. I just try to leave our lines of communication open. I remain sensitive to his feelings, because I did not go through what he has been going through. My parents have been happily married for more than 30 years. The roles were clearly defined in my household. He is acutely aware that in a traditional family make-up I wouldn't play both roles, but he is also aware there is nothing traditional about our family or his mom's profession. He also seems to understand that parenting roles are usually balanced and that I carry the brunt of the balancing on my back. I don't think this negates his experience, if anything I believe he has grown an appreciation for the capabilities of a woman. Thus reinforcing the fact that I could be a role model to him, because I have done extraordinary things in my lifetime. He considers me to be strong and tough and able to do anything the guys can do. With regard to Hip-Hop, he has constant exposure to many female artists so he doesn't view them in a different category. That is right now though,

I'm already strategizing how I will prepare him for the next few years, as he becomes a teen.

Pri: I definitely agree with you. A woman could never teach a man how to be a "man," just a good one. On the other hand, our sons have picked up our creative traits and interests.

Helixx: I know! Nasir tends to do anything and everything I do. I have an adventurous spirit and love extreme sports. I listen to all music from Hip-Hop to heavy metal. Subsequently, by default he loves extreme sports too and also looks up to his dad as well. How did Hip-Hop play a role in your family unit and how did Groovie handle the different transitions that you and his father's relationship went through?

Pri: Well actually the reason why my son's father and I got together in the first place was because of Hip-Hop. We were like seventeen at the time. I was a dancer and MC back then. I wanted to start pursuing Hip-Hop on a larger scale. He had just started DJing and was a Hip-Hop dancer and illustrator as well. I asked him to be my DJ and the magical world of unicorns and love puppets ensued soon after (laughs). Our whole relationship was based around music. Soul and Hip-Hop especially. When Groovie came along it was a creative blessing! His father and I were very young. I was 19 when I became pregnant and I had our son at 20 years old. I really feel like music helped us through my pregnancy and through the challenge of raising a child for the first time. I used to hold headphones to my stomach while I was pregnant and play soul and Hip-Hop tracks. I didn't really think anything of it until one day, when my son was about three weeks old; he was in his crib screaming to the top of his lungs. I was changing his diaper at the time. I couldn't get him to quiet down. I was listening to Maceo Parker and the song "Children's Story" came on. This was the main song I played for him while I was pregnant. He became quiet instantly and began to turn his body towards the speaker, where the sound was coming from. He couldn't focus his eyes yet, but he turned his head towards the sound. After the song was over he began crying again. I was amazed! That let me know how strong the power of music is over us. I used that Maceo Parker song to help soothe him for 13 months, until one day my son got wise and that was a wrap (laughs)! Groovie used to watch his father DJ and became fascinated with the sound the record made while it was scratching. At two years old, he used to sneak out of bed and go into the living room, in the dark mind you, and pull out all of his dad's records from the crates. We would wake up and all the vinyl records would be piled about 100 deep on the Technic turntables, with all of the record covers on the floor and Groovie and our dog at the time, Blue Note, sleeping on top of them (laughs). I love thinking about those days! When his father and I decided to separate, I believe the transition was easier than it could have been, because his father and I were connected creatively and had a lot of love and respect for one another. I learned how to produce music because of his father and then later on I was able to teach Groovie how to make beats because of that. His father and I are close to this day. More like brother and sister now and we still have a Hip-Hop connection. Even now when I speak with Groovie, he will tell me he has a "cool family" and he loves when we all hang out together. I am lucky to have that. Now, since we're on the topic of families, how do you think the Anomolies supported our sons' growth and development?

Helixx: The Anomolies collective is a family. Through thick and thin we are always there for each other. From music to marriage, to heartbreak and deaths, parenthood and Hip-Hop, we stand as a unit. Our children are benefactors of this strong bond. Nas has attended more Anomolies meetings than I can count. He would ask me if he was in Anomolies too. Groovie has also been a permanent fixture at our shows. We take care of one another in and outside of our music and creative circles, so it's only natural that our sons would be a part of that. The Anomolies understand that we are trying to balance music and motherhood. They always do whatever they can to ensure we feel supported. Everyone in the Anomolies is uniquely gifted and talented. Our children are able to leverage the infinite resources that are available within the crew. Big Tara is a b-girl, dance instructor, MC, and style maverick. Kuttin Kandi is our resident DJ/turntablist and writer, who always has incredible insight. Invincible is an MC, who is very connected to the youth through the various organizations she supports.

Pri: In retrospect, if you had the chance to change anything about raising your son within this industry, what would it be?

Helixx: Truthfully, I don't think I would change anything.

Pri: I agree. I feel that everything we have experienced and everything we have shared with our sons has occurred for a reason. Situations, whether positive or negative, are made to mold us as people. Our children have learned how to overcome obstacles based on our keen navigation through this industry. These learned events were vital not only to our kids, but to us as mothers and I would not change a thing. Well, maybe I would change some things (laughs). Like some of those hairstyles and outfits I was rockin' (laughter). Now to close out, let me ask you Helixx, what advice or words of wisdom would you give to any other woman trying to raise children while pursuing a career in the arts? What should they take away from this?

Helixx: I think every woman pursuing a career in Hip-Hop needs a solid support network. Support can come in many shapes and forms. Whether it is through your family, community, friends or peer groups. I think an individual's success is dependent upon the delicate fabric that makes up our social networks. Not just any group of people will do. The people that are part of this network want you to be successful. They want to see you fulfill your dreams. Hip-Hop is an incredible adventure, but it requires tenacity and a fierce commitment to a dream that feels so far away at times. The purpose of a strong network is to support you when the going gets tough. Often when the dream begins to fade, we want to give up. Your network will help you find a way to push through your obstacles. The obstacles never go away, you just don't have to face them alone. What about you Pri?

Pri: Nothing can take away from the experience you will receive as well as the pride you get from pursuing something that you love. I feel that any woman choosing to take this path should definitely be ready for a bumpy ride and if you are a mother, the ride gets even more turbulent. Everything in this journey makes you stronger and every mistake makes you wiser. It is not just about your talent. Your determination, work ethic and the patience you may have developed from being a mother will play a big role in not only keeping you afloat, but in keeping you sane! If it is your dream, pursue it! If that is your choice, you better raise your career like you raise your children! When you do so, eventually your career will listen to you and you will get exactly what you want out of it.

8.
Mothering the Northside

Hip-Hop Mothers North of the 49th Parallel

MAKI MOTAPANYANE AND MARK V. CAMPBELL

THIS CHAPTER WAS MOTIVATED by several factors. First, we noticed that a number of the founding and most active women artists in Canadian Hip-Hop are mothers, and puzzled at the paucity of discussion about motherhood as a formative experience in the relationships that are forged with Hip-Hop. Second, we felt compelled to ask questions about the role of motherhood in shaping the careers of the few mother/artists we knew of who had gained some level of notoriety in the Canadian Hip-Hop industry. Our aim was to begin the process of giving analytical shape to experiences of motherhood in Hip-Hop culture through the reflections of women whose participation in Hip-Hop has involved a negotiation of the interplay between this experience and their artistic lives. In May and October of 2010, we were fortunate to gain interviews with two stalwarts of Canadian Hip-Hop: Lady P, an Emcee whose involvement in Hip-Hop dates back to earlier formative years in this music industry, and Mel Boogie, a DJ managing an active music career in the current Hip-Hop landscape in Canada.

The impetus for this piece was also framed by a six-week community animated exhibition titled *T-Dot Pioneers, An Exploration of Toronto Hip Hop History and Culture*, which was held at the Toronto Free Gallery from March 4 to April 18, 2010. The resounding success of this first historical Hip-Hop exhibit in Canada was in large part due to a panel discussion titled "Where the Ladies @?" Organized by local radio show host and DJ, Mel Boogie, the panel engaged prominent women Hip-Hop artists in an examination of the state of the Hip-Hop industry in Toronto and the place of women artists therein. This panel consisted of Canada's premiere women Hip-Hop artists: Michie Mee, Tara Chase, True Daley, Motion,

Tara Henley, Lady P, Daniela Etienne and DJ L'Oquenz. The narratives that animated this panel discussion also provided the motivation and context for the following two interviews with Lady P and DJ Mel Boogie.

Partnership on this piece has been exceedingly fruitful to our aim of beginning to frame experiences of mothering in the context of Canadian Hip-Hop culture. For his part, Mark Campbell has been active in Toronto's Hip-Hop scene for over a decade, both as a DJ and radio show host—an interest that carried over into his doctoral work. Mark was pivotal in the planning, design, organization and management of the *T-Dot Pioneers* exhibit in Toronto, which I was fortunate to be able to attend with my children. His interviews here with Lady P and DJ Mel Boogie are in line with his wider efforts to document and archive Canadian Hip-Hop history.

My own influence on this piece has centred on understanding the widespread erasure and invisibility of motherhood in Hip-Hop despite the material prominence of this reality in the day-to-day lives of artists, and in the culture more broadly. Having a longstanding interest in women's artistic contributions to North American Hip-Hop culture, I sought the collaboration of a Hip-Hop historian. Questions framing this chapter's semi-structured interviews probed the ways in which women artists link or negotiate their experiences as mothers to their work in Hip-Hop. While the interview questions garnered open-ended answers spanning an array of themes on Canadian Hip-Hop, for the scope of this chapter, we chose the portions of these interviews that best speak to the thematic focus of our piece.

This chapter is structured along two thematic streams: "The Beginning" and "A Woman in Hip-Hop: The Mothering Experience." These streams feature extended portions of the two interviews. The two overarching themes that structure our presentation of interview dialogue were pulled out following a study of the two interviews in their entirety. In the service of brevity and analytical focus, we have organized our present discussion around key portions of the interviews that feature each artist's reflections on their gendered experiences and, more specifically, on the role they may see motherhood playing in their artistry. Although the second thematic stream is composed of two related but different aspects of gendered experience, the artists do not neatly separate these two elements in their interviews. The subject of womanhood and motherhood often appear in the interviews as part of a seamless dialogue about the artist's overall

113

gendered experiences in the Hip-Hop industry. We, therefore, refer to both womanhood and motherhood as gendered experiences in the title to this second section in the aim of more accurately representing the featured portions of the interviews.

In the first section, titled "The Beginning," we examine the early relationship of the two artists to Hip-Hop culture. The artists are asked to describe their most memorable musical influences and to reflect on what and where they learned to participate in Hip-Hop culture. In the second section, "A Woman in Hip-Hop: The Mothering Experience," the dialogue highlights the gendered aspects of the two women's development as artists, and their thoughts on the extent to which this played a formative role in their overall positioning within the Hip-Hop industry. Additionally, the artists speak of the adjustments and shifts that accompanied their transition into motherhood. The interview excerpts appear in order of original recording, with Lady P preceding Mel Boogie. The portions of each artist's interview that correspond to one of the main thematic streams of this chapter follow one another under each thematic heading. Thus, the reader will see that Mel Boogie's comments on her early artistic beginnings appear, distinctly, following Lady P's description of her own. We do the same for the second thematic heading; Mel Boogie's discussion of being a woman artist and a mother in the Hip-Hop industry follows Lady P's narration of her own experiences with gender and motherhood in the context of Hip-Hop. The interview excerpts are placed in context by introductory paragraphs. The names of interview participants appear in the featured excerpts under the initials MC (Mark Campbell), LP (Lady P) and MLB (Mel Boogie). We conclude the chapter with an analysis of what these narratives reveal and how they might serve to nurture on-going dialogue about the dynamically creative force of motherhood in Hip-Hop culture.

THE BEGINNING

Lady P is one of the earliest known female Emcees in Canada, having begun her career with the Kilowatt Soundcrew in the early 1980s. Kilowatt members hailed from the Mississauga region, just outside the Greater Toronto Area, and the crew included MC Fuller G, DJ Carl C, and DJ M&M. Kilowatt was a progressive crew for its time, providing Lady P with an opportunity to rock the crowd while also promoting DJ M&M,

a woman Disc Jockey. Lady P's story is an important one, and not well known in Canada, so her inclusion in this chapter was deliberate. Lady P's impact on the industry has been understated; few are aware of the connection between Toronto's much-celebrated Hip-Hop artist Michie Mee, and Lady P. Lady P was an early role model to Michie Mee, arguably, Canada's most successful female rapper.

DJ Mel Boogie came up in a much different era via the 1990s college radio circuit, beginning her career on the *Break-A-Dawn* show on CHRY 105.5 FM. As the younger sister of Maestro Fresh Wes, Canada's first platinum Hip-Hop artist, Mel Boogie's journey and access to the industry differ significantly from Lady P's. Currently, Mel Boogie is part of the Droppin' Dimes crew on CKLN 88.1 FM, Canada's only all-woman Hip-Hop radio show.[1] Mel Boggie's résumé is strong with appearances and gigs including Toronto's annual 416 Graffiti Expo, the North by NorthEast Indie Showcase, and the Woman 2 Woman Expo. She has also appeared as a speaker and panelist at a variety of music industry conferences. Mel Boogie has opened for Busta Rhymes, Q-Tip, M.O.P., Rah Digga, and countless other major Hip-Hop acts. Women DJs on Toronto's Hip-Hop scene are rare, often numbering less than a handful in each generation. In this context, Mel Boogie's success is noteworthy. The following section examines the two artists' early beginnings in Hip-Hop.

LADY P'S EARLY BEGINNING IN HIP-HOP

Before Hip-Hop as we know it emerged as a viable commercial industry, the scene was a plethora of young creative talent expressed via graffiti art, DJing and especially b-boying/b-girling. High school events and roller skating rinks were the two arenas where Hip-Hop's creative spirit could be witnessed and experienced regularly. Lady P's recollection of her earliest rhymes is connected to a high school basketball game. For a first generation Guyanese-Canadian woman, Lady P's social outings necessarily involved a male relative's accompaniment, and often included various cousins and siblings. In the early 1980s, Hip-Hop music and culture were still very embryonic, such that identity for many young Afro-Caribbean Canadian youth had not yet coalesced around a clear articulation of their belonging within Hip-Hop culture.

MC: Do you have a childhood influenced by Hip-Hop culture? If yes, what did it look like? Was it being played around you? How did Hip-Hop affect you as a young person?

LP: As a young person it affected me because it gave me the opportunity to be able to express myself as a female going out there and getting on a stage and speaking and it helped, in a weird way, public speaking. Because you have to think about what you're gonna write, you have to think about what you're gonna say, you have to also know your audience.

MC: Was there any influences that were from the Caribbean?

LP: You know what? There were. It was more of the reggae singers, female reggae singers. Back in the day then, for me, you didn't really see many female rappers, but you saw a Lady Saw, who would go out there and chat. So back in my day, there wasn't really that many female Emcees but you saw a lot of females like Marcia Griffiths.

MC: Nana Maclean? I think she might have been in Toronto.

LP: Yup, Nana Maclean. But I had the opportunity in 2007 to actually meet Lady Saw and to tell her how much she influenced me because, just remembering her going on the stage and being empowered to go up there and ... go up there to sing, but also to chat, to rap.

MC: I wouldn't have guessed Lady Saw.

LP: Yup, yup, that was one of my influences. And also, here, when I was younger, listening to different speeches and stuff like that. We used to have Black history sessions at Overly, way back in the day, where you could go in and listen to public speakers like Dudley Laws and those guys come in and speak, and they would do it in kind of a chant form and all that. So there was a mixture of influences, both Canada and the Caribbean.

MC: At what point did you realize that "I have to be part of Hip-Hop?"

LP: I can't remember the year, but actually, it's funny 'cause I was singing one of the rhymes today at work. Just recognizing that people can put words together and it have a melody, and it's also a party theme. Back then, for me it was sports. So it was going to basketball games and track and field and football, and we were allowed to back then, we were able to take our ghetto blasters to the game. We didn't have a dollar store back then, so you had to go and everybody would put in their money and buy ten batteries 'cause you could only use batteries in them in those days. And it was a battle that encouraged me to get into it is, in the beginning at my high school in Mississauga, Clarkson high school, we literally had one section where the blacks were, and another section where the whites

116

were. So we'd come in, if a basketball team was coming in from a rival school, we'd put together our music and have our music blasting, make sure everybody chipped, take their lunch money and buy our batteries. And we started blasting our music in the cafeteria. And at lunchtime, or after school or before the game. Then the white kids would come and have their rock. So it was R&B or dance music, and they'd have their rock. And the only way that we were able to shut them down is when rap music started to come out.

MC: Oh really?

LP: Yup, so for example, Sugar Hill Gang and Grand Master Flash and those guys. And one of the songs that I really enjoyed was the "Don't-push-me-'cause-I'm-close-to-the-edge," right? So we would go back and forth, so it was rap against rock. So I liked the way that was flowing and I liked the way the words were going, and one day I was just hanging over at Carl who was a DJ then for Kilowatts,[2] and we were just hanging around and his school was TL Kennedy, my school was Clarkson, and we were having a basketball game against each other, and he was playing music and stuff like that and I just lay on the floor and I just wrote, my very first rap was about basketball, it was about Clarkson beating TL Kennedy, I can't even remember it. But it was about basketball players and everything 'cause I had this huge crush on this guy who played at his (Carl's) school, and he was a basketball player and my first rap was about basketball and I started writing it and … I recognized that that was a way that we could get our message out, put it out on cassette tape, and blast it and play it back.

MC: So you, your first rap was actually recorded?

LP: My first rap was on a cassette tape, yup.

MEL BOOGIE'S EARLY BEGINNING IN HIP-HOP

In the 1990s, Hip-Hop had emerged as a cultural force, post-Public Enemy and during a time when Toronto had already been blessed with the artistry of Michie Mee, Rumble & Strong and Maestro Fresh Wes. Like Lady P, as a young Afro-Guyanese woman in Canada, Mel Boogie's early beginnings in Hip-Hop also involved a male relative's presence.

MC: Could you talk a little bit about your earliest years in which Hip-Hop was part of your youth, or when it first influenced you?

MLB: Rappers Delight, and back then my dad had gotten my brother and I our own turntables 'cause he didn't want us playing on his stuff ... yeah, it was mainly just to keep the children off of his stuff and that's kind of where it started. And then once my older brother[3] started getting into Emceeing and we started listening to Ron Nelson, Ron is probably one of the biggest influences for me as far as getting into radio.

MC: Okay. So Ron Nelson then became a really big influence for you.

MLB: Yeah, yeah, exactly. So, yeah, growing up, college radio, actually CKLN[4] was very important to me so, when I actually started having a show there it meant that much more to me. As far as early beginnings that's how I first fell in love with Hip-Hop ... for me ... I didn't just kinda say, "yeah, I wanna DJ or become a DJ or do radio." It was just kind of an evolution of sorts, like throughout high school I listened to all the stuff like I'm sure you listened to like, you know, Black Moon and Nice n' Smooth and Native Tongues. And when Rap City[5] was on TV, I used to watch that religiously; my parents were really strict so I wasn't allowed to go out anywhere. So even though, you know, Wes was out performing and doing his thing—"Let Your Back Bone Slide"[6] came out when I was in the ninth grade, so, it made for an interesting high school experience. But seeing him as an artist and that kind of thing made me realize that I, as much as I love Hip-Hop and I want to contribute to it, I don't like the stage that much being the centre of attention that much, but DJing and being in the background but still contributing, that kind of appealed to me. Of course, nowadays it's different because the DJs are, you know, you're kind of forced to be in the spotlight, but back then, that's ... that's what I was aiming for.

MC: So, would you say there was a double standard by the time you were in grade nine that, you know, Wes was much older but you know, if you were his age they probably wouldn't let you go out the same way?

MLB: Oh no, they wouldn't let me go out the same way. There's always a double standard, it's a West Indian home, so you know, the girl child must stay home. Like even up to now my mom just recently started accepting the fact that I'm a DJ and like I've won awards, and like, when she saw me at *E-Talk Daily,*[7] pardon me?

MC: Your Moms just recognizing that you gotta be out there, you got a career, you gotta be outta the house too just like...

MLB: Right, right. And I mean when I first started getting into it and playing out in clubs and stuff, I was in my early twenties. I started doing radio when I was 19, so kinda around that age is when I started doing club stuff too. And I guess, you know, as a parent you don't want your daughter to be up in the clubs all the time, all kinda hours, but yeah, over the years she's softened, both my parents have come to accept it.

MC: But it took work on your end right, like you just had to keep pushing along and...

MLB: Yeah, it's still taking work because now that I'm a parent I have to work extra hard to show why I'm doing it. For me it's kinda two fold because it's a hobby, it's something that I really really love and it's something that's exclusively for me, like it's just for mommy, it's my thing that I do on my own, and the other side of that is I like to be able to contribute to the evolution of or the development of some kind of foundation in Canada because being Maestro's sister I had I guess a special seat in witnessing the types of struggles that artists go through. We don't have a foundation here for Wes who came out 20 years ago when rap was just seen as a trend, and they thought, you know, it wasn't gonna last as long as it did ... he kinda made a way when there was no way. So for me, seeing him go through all that and me being a DJ on radio I wanted to have some kind of impact in making that journey easier for artists so that's why I do what I do. And my mom and my dad slowly come to accept that, they're not, you know, one hundred percent, but, at this point they're like, she's been doing this for long so I guess she's not gonna give it up so we might as well support her.

MC: So, so you've been on the radio, is it eight years now on Droppin' Dimez?

MLB: I've been on Droppin' Dimez ten years this year, but I used to be on CHRY with DJ Manifest.[8]

Mel Boogie and Lady P are from two very different eras when we begin to think about the public visibility and viability of Hip-Hop as a cultural phenomenon. Lady P's early explorations with rapping came at a time when no other women in Canada were known to be rapping in any kind of organized fashion. With this being said, Lady P's presence in the early days of Hip-Hop was part of a larger more visible contingent of women in Hip-Hop from Roxanne Shanté to Toronto's DJ M&M (mentioned earlier) and a plethora of other women, Fly K and Mischievous C for example, whose association to Hip-Hop has waned over the years.

By the mid-1990s when DJ Mel Boogie was just coming up in the industry, the public visibility of women in Hip-Hop was a much more filtered and controlled image. It was increasingly women's bodies rather than their skills that were the product of consumption. It is of significant note that Mel Boogie's efforts to become a successful DJ took place primary through a non-visual medium, the radio. As Mel Boogie mentions in her interview, she refuses to be visually consumed and highlights her "sweatpants and shelltoes" as her defiant Hip-Hop dress code.

A WOMAN IN HIP-HOP: THE MOTHERING EXPERIENCE

As authors of a piece that speaks to our love of Hip-Hop culture and history, we lament the ways in which the indelible marks that women such as Sylvia Robinson[9] left on Hip-Hop culture, would be eroded over time by an unrelenting male-centeredness and disfiguring commercialization. In a less commercialized Hip-Hop era, during the early and mid 1970s, it was common to rate men and women Hip-Hoppers on a multifaceted skill set including rhyming skills, dancing skills, originality and "freshness' (admittedly, the most subjective criterion). The success of the Kilowatt Soundcrew is a testament to these early criteria for status and success. Lady P highlights this as she recollects playing parties with various sound crews.

LADY P ON GENDER, MOTHERING AND HIP-HOP

LP: Back then it was just, it was for fun and doing the basketball rap and then the UFTO concert came up and then after a while the guys were like "Pen, you really can do this"… and then it got to a point where we had the battles. So the first battle was against Sunshine Soundcrew[10] and it was at, oh gosh, this club at, this club or hall that we rented out and it was Sunshine, it was Maceo Soundcrew … they would all be scratching and doing all this stuff and all that and they'd have their Emcees … and then my guys would put me on the mic.

MC: And you'd tear it down?

LP: Yeah.

MC: Does that mean none of the other crews had women rapping for them?

LP: None of the other crews had women rapping.… I definitely wanna pay homage to Fly K and my other cousin Mischievous C[11].… Because they were out there, they'd write the raps, they'd be all ready and then as soon as it's time to get on the stage, they're like "uh uh, I can't do it."

MC: So at what point in the journey then, you said Cordell came in '86, so how many years before that, were you rhyming at parties and doing battles?

LP: Cordell came in '86 but I was rhyming since '81.... So from when I started rapping in '81 and it was a whirlwind ... all over, like we used to do ... Montreal, I was pregnant then, I was about six months pregnant. We did Juneteenth, which used to be an open concert in Buffalo, New York; it was a hip-hop/R&B version of Caribana.[12] And we literally rented a cube van and put all of our equipment in the back of the cube van and drove across the border, went to Juneteenth, turned the van around, opened it up, Carl hooked up the mic and everything and I just started rappin'.

MC: So did motherhood kind of changed everything or...?

LP: Well what happened is, well I found out I was pregnant, and I mean, that didn't stop me. Before that I was rapping all over the place any place that there was an opportunity for a dance or a gig, we were there. Then I found out I was pregnant, and I was still going out, like on Caribana weekend and whenever they had like a club or a party or whatever and I'd get an opportunity, I'd get on the mic.

MC: What was the reaction of everyone, like Kilowatt?

LP: Well it's funny 'cause Marcia[13] and I—it was like four of us, so we were like four best friends, so two, I hate the word babyfather, so two fathers, Carl and Courtney, and myself and Marcia, so Marcia had a son for Carl, I had a son for Courtney. So it was all in the group. And what was the reaction? Well Cordell's father and I—which we're no longer together—he became kind of like, you know, "I don't want my child mother out there doin' this and that whatever." And then my parents were like, you know, "you shouldn't be out there rappin' and you should go find a decent job" and do all this kind of stuff ... and basically, I still continued going. I'd leave my son with my mom and dad ... we did Heavens night club ... I rapped with—and I was actually pregnant but I didn't realize I was pregnant—Fresh Prince, Will Smith and Jazzy Jeff, Whodini. The guys body surfed me and put me up on the stage with Whodini, and I started doing their friend's rap and did it in my own version, so the reaction was positive and negative. Positive in the sense of I let family and obviously my child's father convince me that this isn't gonna go anywhere, these guys ain't gonna do nothin' with female Emcees. And then I went through some stuff with my ex and I ended up leaving the country, and going to, and living in California for a year and a half with my son. This is in 1988, as I was getting on the plane, I called and checked my voicemail and Ron Nelson[14] was like, "Pen you've gotta come out to this thing, these guys are gonna be there, this is gonna be the break that you wanted" ... but I was just getting ready to go on the plane. So, without dishing the dirty, my son's father knew that Ron Nelson and those guys were getting ready to kind of get me, and Maestro's told me this too, that he was like, "Pen you just disappeared, 'cause we had some stuff ready for ya...." But I like to position this in a positive way, because you know what, you can't hold on to that, you gotta move forward, right? So I always say when anyone asks, I say I gave up my mic for baby booties. And it's the best thing that I did at that time and it was the right thing I did at that time because of my son. My son and I went away to California for a year and a half, came back, and I raised him as a single mother. When I came back I hooked up with Ron Nelson, and he hooked me up with another guy who shall remain nameless, who is very much in the business, and I mean, you see him all around, he's very much in the business, and I almost started to come back. So this was ... '89 ... and hooked up with Ron Nelson, and was like, you know, "I wanna get back in the business, I wanna do it, like, these guys told me there was an opportunity, I see how Wes[15] is blown up, what can you do for me?" So Ron's like, "Pen, I'm gonna hook you up with this guy," thinkin' he's cool—and, the guy said to me "yeah yeah yeah, we can do this, we're gonna change your name to MC Duchess," and I said "Yeah, well, it's just me and my son," and he said, "Yeah, leave your son with somebody and I'll come pick you up about two o'clock in the morning."

MC: What?

LP: Yeah, and I'm like writing all this stuff and I'm like "I'm ready, I'm ready', and he's like, "Yeah, Ok that's good but we gotta work on it together" ... and you know, I wasn't willing to meet him at very weird hours 'cause it was just me hustling with my son, and then he just kind of faded away. And then I just came straight out and said, "What is in this for you?" And he was pretty straight with what it was, so I was just like you know what, forget it.

MC: Yeah, too shady, too creepy.

LP: And like I said, he's still around, and he's still in the business and he's done a lot. Like I see him do stuff with Michie, and that kind of stuff, so whatever.

MC: The position you have now is, like, the godmother, the godmother of Canadian Hip-Hop, still ... the way things have worked out, I'm really glad personally that these kinds of stories are coming out.

LP: And this is why I pay homage to Michie, because, between my cousin Kwame, who I don't know if you met him, but anyways, he was with FLOW,[16] through me, when I was in California I was calling Ron Nelson saying, "look, I got a little cousin who at twelve and thirteen, I used to sneak him into the dances" and ... they grew up coming to dances, like, our dances that we'd have. And I would sneak them in and get them to carry the crates and all that kind of stuff and they would stand behind the turn tables and watch the guys DJ ... like, they were only allowed to go out 'cause they were going out with their big cousin Penny. At the Stylus Awards[17] where we were inducted, he was the one who presented us with out award, and.... He said "if it wasn't for my cousin, like ... our family, you know West Indian family, everybody was like "go get a proper job" ... he stuck to the music and he's been on all the top radio stations. And he was like "if it wasn't for my cousin and this group Kilowatt, I wouldn't have known anything about turntables and music and all these kinda different people." And I'm so proud of him 'cause he's taken it to the next level where he's at the BET Awards interviewing these people, you know what I mean? But why I brought him in is, if it wasn't for him and Michie and a few other people continuing to keep my name alive—and she's constantly paying homage—with regards to how she got into it too and seeing me at shows and stuff like that, like, she was a little young'un, not that much younger, but young enough where she would come to the shows and stuff like that and she was, people don't know this, but she originally started with Sunshine[18] with my cousin Butch Lee. Her brother was a DJ for Sunshine.

MC: So besides the T-Dot Pioneers panel discussion, have you noticed if anyone really talks about motherhood as part of Hip-Hop culture?

LP: Not really, and that kind of disappoints me, because even though, sitting on the panel I realize it's still a very huge part of it ... there's still a lot of single mothers out there trying to hustle and grind and do what they gotta do and I think it needs to be brought to the forefront because it just shows the strength of us as women what we can do and how far we can go with it. Like, with me being a mother and being in Hip-Hop, my son was a track and field runner, he's got Canadian track and field championships, he went away to school on a scholarship, he came back—and he's got tattoos—but the tattoos on his arm, which I don't like ... one of them is headphones with a cord and the cord goes into like, it looks like it's going into his vein, and in that it says "music's in my blood." That's what he claims he did for me for mother's day.

MC: Oh really, without your blessing, right?

LP: Yeah, and then he has on his wrist, Lady P ... my point to that is that as mothers, we need to embrace the fact that—and not go out there and glorify the single mother status and all that, and this is coming from a single mother—but glorify a woman that is out there in a business that is male dominated, we're still trying to get our hustle and still trying to influence the next generation, and be mother's to the next generation. And how do you do it? How do you stay strong? And also not compromise your integrity?

MC: It's about time that people have these conversations as part of Hip-Hop, right?

LP: Yeah yeah, exactly.

MC: Now, what do you think, what do you hope would sort of come out of, this interview is going to be put together with another interview from a mother in Toronto's Hip-Hop scene.

LP: You should also get Mel Boogie. Mel Boogie is Maestro Fresh Wes' sister. She's got two children and she's just, I, I admire her.

MC: She's grinding right now. You know what? Funny you should say, she called me this, couple of weeks ago and she's like, "are you planning on putting on *Where Da Ladies At panel?*" and I was like, I don't know yet. I'm planning my event for June and she wants to do it in March, so I was like, "yeah, go ahead and do it, I'll help you, but you can take it over," so that looks like it's gonna happen each year now. And she's doing this with her, I think she has three kids, and she works full time and she does a radio show.

LP: And she's out all over, DJing, promoting, I mean, she was at Honey Jam.[19] She's a must, from the female DJ aspect and also, what got her into it, you know, her brother, he's an icon.

MC: So, what would be some of the things you would hope would come out of this book? I mean, one thing for sure that I can say will come out of this book is that in the U.S. colleges and universities Hip-Hop studies is a growing area, right? And they definitely will be using this book in those classes. But beyond that ...

LP: Well, what I would like to come out of this is that, I don't know if you saw on BET they had, basically, *Where Da Ladies At?* but they had it with, like, MC Lyte they even paid homage to Lauryn Hill, and reminded us all, you know, she's got a beautiful voice and everything like that, but she started rapping, she was a rapper ... I'd like to see that, I'd like to see this book into Canadian schools.

MEL BOOGIE ON GENDER, MOTHERING AND HIP-HOP

MC: So at what point in your journey were you, like, okay, I'm ready to become a mother and I can reconcile these two things, you know what I mean? Because it's starving artist and, you know, overworked mom are two of not the most compatible things.

MLB: Right, it didn't really happen that way, my thought process was not like that at all. I met my husband at CHRY 'cause he had a show there, and yeah, when we were surprised with what soon came to be Xavier. My parents were, they just thought that because I was having a baby and gonna be a mom that I would stop DJing, stop doing radio, and it just never happened. There really wasn't a thought process where I had to say okay, I'm gonna balance the two and reconcile the two, it was just, this is what I love doing, I'm a parent first, but I love doing this, so being a parent is my priority and I'm still gonna be making time in my life for this because I have that much passion for it.

MC: So did you have to take some time off for the next year or say I can't really do the show, did it end up like that?

MLB: With Xavier I did take some time off, I can't remember how long. With Kiana I definitely did as well, I took, well CHRY was actually going through some changes around the time that I had Kiana so *Break-A-Dawn* was no more, we lost our show and I was looking for another home as far as radio was concerned. So about five months after I had Kiana, I bumped into Lindsay, who was just taking over Droppin' Dimez from Jemini 'cause she moved over to FLOW 93.5, this was back in 2001, and she asked me to come through and do a guest spot, and I never left. With my last son I only took off, maybe like eight months all together? So in the past ten years I've only been off radio for eight months.

MC: So how did people respond—people that were booking you for clubs and the dudes that you were hangin' out with or even your crew. Were people kind of like, oh third child and all, probably not coming back, or something like that?

MLB: Yeah, there were a few people who said that but the people who know me well, know me well enough to know that I'm not, I, I don't give up easily, and especially something like this which is important to me it only makes me work that much harder. As far as like, mothering and being a woman in this type of industry, I never really set out to, how can I describe it, to prove that "yeah, women can do it." It's just, for me personally, it's just something that I love to do and because I love to do it I'm gonna make it work for me.

MC: Did you find, maybe, after each child, you got more hungry to stay in the DJing scene? Was it like, "it's gonna be so much harder to balance this and now I can't wait to get back to the turntables," or "I can't wait to get back to my show and get back into it kind of thing?" Also, how did your experience as a mother then influence your DJing career going forward; was there a major impact?

MLB: It's a major impact in terms of being able to balance it all because it's not easy as a parent, you know that, whether you're a mom or a dad and you're a dedicated parent, you know, it's not easy to balance all of it. At the end of the day your kids have to be your priority. It's worked out for me where the show that I'm on right now is late enough that, I'm home to like cook dinner and help them with their homework, get them ready for bed before I even leave, so I put them to bed and then I leave, and when they wake up I'm home.

MC: You also have a full-time job too, right? You also go to work in the daytime

MLB: Yeah, I got a full-time job and I do PR on the side.

MC: But your husband's really supportive then, because was he a Hip-Hop DJ?

MLB: Yeah, yeah, he used to DJ so he understands, he has his moments where he's like, "Okay, seriously Mel, like c'mon." But for the most part he's really supportive, and I think it's because he used to DJ that he understands.

MC: Yeah, not a lot, not enough women have that kind of support from their partner.

MLB: Exactly.

MC: Just knowing that he has first hand knowledge and love of exactly what you're doing, right?

MLB: Right, exactly. And I mean he went through his phases where he was playing out all the time and stuff and I was the one at home taking care of the kids, so, it's just a matter of it being, you know, busy for me right now, so, I mean that's what a relationship is supposed to be, right? Give and take, so fortunately it's worked out. Fourteen years later.

MC: Fourteen years? You've been married for fourteen years?

MLB: Yeah. This year's fourteen years.

MC: And how long you been DJing?

MLB: Since 1993 yeah, before then it was just foolin' around here and there. I was good friends with Agile[20] in high school; I used to go over to his house, like, all the time, he used to let me practice on his turntables, but I wouldn't have considered myself, I wouldn't have called myself a DJ then. It was probably just when I got on radio. And of course, 'cause it's college radio, you learn on the air. You make mistakes, and you know, you have to work to improve, so I basically learned how to play on the air.

MC: So then, how did you make a transition to live shows, how did that come about? Did people just sort of recognize you from your radio slot?

MLB: Well pretty much people just recognized me from the radio show, or they'd be looking for a female DJ and the novelty of a female DJ, and I was the one, one of the few in the city who was representing at that level and able to play in clubs and on radio so, after a while people just started recognizing my name. And it's only now, like, 20 years later that I'm actually trying to focus more on the business end of it as opposed to the artist, DJing, culture end of it. For the first time I have a manager now and two years ago that would have been unheard of for me. But it's just because the whole perception of what a DJ is and is supposed to do has changed. It's not good enough just to, you know, rock a party and do a good job at that, or have a stellar formatted show. People want to see the flash and glitz, but as far as I'm concerned there's no flash and glitz, I'm like jogging suit and shell toes all day, you know what I mean? But you know, you *have* to have a website, you *have* to have online presence.

MC: And that's really changed the game since the early years, even late '90s. Click used to ask me when I first got on radio, "why don't you get a website?" I'm like, I can't afford that! That's crazy, only like, Fortune 500 companies have websites, now I got three.

MLB: Well now it's a necessity, like you have to have some kind of online presence and I'm behind the game with that because I've tried to resist it for as long as possible. Unlike a lot of the female DJs out there I don't practice modelling on the side. I don't look at myself in the mirror and practice poses. Not to down play that, I meant, that's an important part of the game now, but I mean, my focus is learning the music and trying to play properly instead of what kind of fashion brands are gonna be sponsoring me. But that's all a part of the game so, either you play or you don't kind of thing.

MC: I actually just pulled up this email today that you're gonna be on this panel with Michie Mee for Canadian Music Week.[21] How was T-Dot Pioneers, how was that panel for you in terms of, last year we generated a whole lot of buzz, and there was a lot of people that came out to listen and a lot of people got to talk about their experiences as a woman in Hip-Hop, but there was also some important, like I just recently posted an important clip from Michie Mee where she talks about being a mother and the struggles of being a mother while in Hip-Hop culture. Is there, do you find that there's lots of spaces to discuss motherhood?

MLB: No, there isn't.

MC: Even just amongst women in Hip-Hop, it's not a topic that you bond around?

MLB: No, no, not at all. And it's weird, you might have some one-on-one conversations but in terms of having a panel where you get to talk to guys and girls of different ages in different areas of their lives about what it's like to have that balance and to work through that struggle to accomplish what you want to accomplish, we don't discuss it enough. I wouldn't say being a mother will hold you back, but the realistic part of it is if you're going to be a parent, you're going to have to sacrifice, whether Hip-Hop is a part of the picture or not, as a parent you sacrifice. Sometimes you have to put what you wanna do off to the side for the betterment of your kids. And I mean, in hindsight, yeah, there are probably a lot of opportunities that I did have to let go of because my kids are my priority. My youngest is five now and I've only just started travelling to play out. It's because I really feel that I should be here for them. But then can I do a six-month tour around the world right now? No. But a weekend here or there, that can probably run, and as they get older I'll be able to do a little bit more. But they're the priority right now and I don't think it's just something that people don't think about. Like for a male DJ to have to become a parent there is an impact on his life, but there's not necessarily an impact on his career. That's the difference. As much as Women's Lib says, you know, you can have it all and we're equal, we're not equal. You know? You're a husband, you can see that, you know, I'm sure that you're a very giving husband and you do a lot for your children but your wife does stuff as a mother that you're not able to do, and that's just life.

MC: One of the reasons I took on this project is 'cause you know I do a lot of academic work around Hip-Hop. And I just thought, like, we need to have, after, you know, being at the panel that you organized[22] and sitting with another two hundred people in that room … I'm thinking, this is such an important topic that we don't get to talk about enough, because if we did get to talk about it more, people would understand Hip-Hop in an entirely different light. You know what I mean? Like, the love and the passion for the creative element of your life that you have, you know, mothers that have to go through all of these things just to be a part of Hip-Hop culture. You got some dudes that get all the shine where it's like, all they do is rhyme about crack or guns or whatever, fizzle out in a year or two … but yet you've got this undercurrent of people that are struggling to just be a part of the culture because it enriches your life and makes you happy. So I thought that, this is why I jumped on this project, because, this is a book on mothering and Hip-Hop culture, but it's gonna be used to teach Hip-Hop culture across the United States and Canada, and I thought, you know, it's yourself and Lady P that's in here, and I wanted to make sure that there's representation not just from the rappers but from other elements of the culture. And I felt like we don't have these discussions enough, there's a lot of all these discussions about feminism and Hip-Hop and misogyny in Hip-Hop which are good and fine and well needed but at the same time, if we start talking about mothers we shift the whole balance of the discussion away from like guns and gangs and bravado and we start talking about real people and real lives and love for the culture. You know what I mean? And the next stop is fatherhood, right? Like, men are gonna have to talk about being, learning to be fathers while, you know, trying to be in the rap game, this and that kind of thing.

MLB: And balancing that. Because you know, with the whole male bravado that comes along with being an Emcee. For a lot of Emcees out there, not for all of them, when you have a daughter, how can you, how do you balance talking about certain things when you have a daughter who's growing up and you're like the number one star in their life. And even as a DJ, yeah, I go through that too because we play pretty grimy stuff considering it's an all-female show but we also play a lot of conscious stuff, we play a lot of female artists, we have a lot of independent artists come through. So for us there's a balance, but as a parent, I still censor what my kids listen to and what they watch. We don't have BET[23] it's just because personally I find that the images plus the music is just a lot to interpret. So even when we do watch videos, like if we're watching something on MUCH[24] or something on *Rap City* together or whatever, I want them to be introduced to what I love but I have to explain to them some of the stuff isn't real. Most of it isn't real. You know? And you have to use your brain to decipher what they're really tryin' to tell you what they're tryin' to sell you, and, and, what it is you're taking away from that.

MC: And, just to add to that, to me, having these discussions with your kids, and having real, honest open discussions about Hip-Hop culture is just that much easier when you start talking about being a mother and being part of Hip-Hop culture because that's real. You know what I mean? And, when that's on the table then we don't really need to be talking about Maybach music and this kind of foolish stuff around consumerism whatever, when there's a real discussion happening with real people that are saying this is really my life, and this is what I really go through to be part of this.

MLB: Yeah. But you know what? All that stuff, the Maybach music and all that kind of grizzly stuff, that's always been a part of Hip-Hop. Always, always, you know, parties, having fun.

MC: It has. But the thing is, it hasn't always been the major focus. And I feel like everybody's focusing on that and we gotta try and shift the balance of what we're focusing on. I mean the whole Hip-Hop industry is way different, right? So you know back in the days when people had Adidas suits and all that it was the same thing is kinda what we're seeing now on a smaller scale, right? But you still had your Public Enemys and your Jungle Brothers. But it's just harder now for your kids to see a diversity of imagines you know? Even someone like Talib Kweli who's huge, right, it's just harder to get that message to you.

MLB: There's no balance. That's the problem that I have. So people coming up today, the youngsters coming up today, they just see, you know, teach me how to Dougie. They don't see the Talib Kwelis or they don't see the Commons. Like, I'm sure there's younger Emcees who are conscious but we don't hear about them. And that's the problem that I have with Hip-Hop today. I'm cool with the teach me how to Dougies, like, it's fun, you know, Hip-Hop is fun, but, like if that's all you see, then that's not real. Like, life isn't just about fun, there's serious stuff that goes on too. There's thought provoking stuff. Like, for Hip-Hop, for me, listening to Public Enemy made me wanna read more, read about Malcolm X. What other kind of music does that?

MC: I know, I can honestly say half of my vocab I learned from Hip-Hop, from Nas, specifically, 'cause I would learn a word from him and then go look it up. You couldn't get me to look that word up in school, not for the life of me. But if Nas was rhyming that word? I was gonna go figure out what it meant. But just to wrap up, the last sort of area I wanted to touch on is, what would be your hopes and dreams for a book like this? You know, a collection of essays from across North America in terms of anybody that's interested in learning about Hip-Hop culture, what would you want them to take away from a book like this?

MLB: I'd want them to understand that women in Hip-Hop have more than just one role. We're Emcees, we're DJs, we're producers but also, as, as a parent, being a parent is my top priority, but my love for Hip-Hop is something that keeps me going. When I was pregnant I was on bed rest.

MC: Oh my.

MLB: Yeah, and that's for like my last two pregnancies I was on bed rest. So that's all I could think about was getting back into it and having that one thing that's just for me. Because, like you said, I work from 9:00 to 5:00, I come home, my Mondays especially, work from 9:00 to 5:00 do the newsletter for the show, cook dinner, help the kids with their homework and all that, up until like 9:30, then I practice for the show, leave at 10:30 and on the air from 11:00 pm to 2:00 am. And that's my Monday. So, I haven't even slept yet. Like last night a young cat came to the studio, he had some questions about getting into the industry and, me, I have a hard time telling people no, so we ended up talking until 3:30 in the morning and I had to start work at 8:30 this morning so, yeah, no sleep. But it's the love that kind of eases the pain a bit? Knowing that I'm contributing somehow, or impacting somehow the industry is what's important. For me, at the end of the day I wanna be able to know that I, this was for something. Like all this time? 'cause it's all volunteer work, like, I get paid to play out but I'm not getting, like, Starting From Scratch[25] money, I'm getting Mel Boogie money let's be real. So, I want to have some type of impact and be able to, to say that I made some kind of difference and I helped some people get somewhere, and I helped build something here, 'cause I find it's too easy for people just to sit back and complain about what we don't have, well get up and do something about it.

THE SHIFTING CRAFT: READING THE NARRATIVES

Emcee Lady P and DJ Mel Boogie's narratives speak to different eras in Hip-Hop culture. Their stories, nonetheless, reveal thought-provoking connections. The interviews indicate that Diasporic musical influences, particularly the work of women artists in Hip-Hop, reggae, and dance-hall among other genres, played an important role in their early creative self-visioning as women Hip-Hop artists in Canada. At the same time, the conversations about early artistic beginnings also reveal that women's practical beginnings in Hip-Hop often take place through tutelage by or connections to men already involved in the industry. Both Lady P and Mel Boogie's early beginnings were sustained through their links to male artists—a DJ friend and a successful rapper brother (among other men in the industry), respectively. Gender was a factor with which both women artists had to contend in their early formation, and the sexist attitudes of family members and work acquaintances would continue to shape their experiences in the music industry. Pregnancy itself did not prove a barrier to artistic production for either artist, though importantly, both women characterize the Hip-Hop business as male-dominated, necessitating diverse strategies of negotiation—from remaining confident and not succumbing to sexism, to taking advantage of the gaps that sexism leaves in the industry as a means of promoting oneself as a novelty act. Lady P continued to perform in shows for the duration of her pregnancy, and Mel Boogie's short breaks from music occurred after the births of her children.

It is following their children's births that both women really faced the challenge of fighting for an artistic place in the Hip-Hop industry. Interestingly, both women attribute a significant portion of this challenge to their struggle to overcome the fixed ideas of family members regarding appropriate behaviour and pursuits for mothers. In both cases, Hip-Hop gigs and the music industry standard of active self-promotion did not meet the approval of Lady P's partner or Mel Boogie's parents as appropriate endeavours for the new mothers. While their artistic pursuits may have been encouraged (in the case of the former, by her partner) or tolerated (in the case of the latter, by her parents), the arrival of the babies signalled, in the estimation of these influential family members, the need for a shift away from the dynamism of the Hip-Hop industry towards maternal respectability and a certain level of piety. Evidently, both artists had to contend with the unfortunate assumption on the part of family members that responsible mothering is diametrically opposed to an artistic life in Hip-Hop.

For Lady P, tensions in her personal relationship with her son's father, and pressure from family in the early 1980s contributed significantly to her decision to move out of the country, in effect, breaking the wave of music opportunities that were slowly gathering for her. She never managed to recover from this stagnation in her music career, despite a later attempt to resuscitate what she had left behind in Toronto upon returning from California. Her bid towards reinvention failed to get off the ground after she was placed in the charge of an established male figure in the industry who did not take her talent or career seriously, and sought to pre-empt any serious work on her behalf with a sexual relationship. This experience, among others, leads Lady P to characterize the Hip-Hop music industry as a male dominated space in which women constantly negotiate their "integrity." Her experience resonates with Hip-Hop scholar Tricia Rose's assessment that, often, women engaged in such negotiations are "struggling for parity, fighting to be taken seriously in a music industry that has a horrible reputation for tolerating and participating in the abuse, sexual harassment, and sexist containment of women artists and employees" (Rose 170). Retrospectively, it is her family and her ex-partner that Lady P thinks got the best of her where her music career is concerned, though she imbues her reading of the past with personal agency when she notes that *she* prioritized motherhood and "gave up [her] mic for baby booties." This statement is interesting in that Lady P considers her past decisions as "the best thing that I did *at that time* ... the right thing I did *at that time*." As she tells her interviewer, she prefers to read past decisions positively. Nevertheless, the sense of missed opportunities lingers heavily over the interview, framed by her one, unsuccessful effort to revive her music career in the early '90s. The motherhood *or* Hip-Hop premise for women artists' choices appears to have been a more prevalent consideration in Lady P's narrative.

Mel Boogie, for her part, has managed to maintain a steady presence in the Hip-Hop community over the years. She notes the gendered double standard that her parents applied to her endeavours towards artistic development in contrast to the leniency shown her brother. Her late night gigs at clubs, a staple of a DJ's professional development, were met with a resistance on the domestic front that Mel Boogie attributes to her parents' West-Indian inflected notions of propriety for young women. It is worthy of note that although Mel Boogie's parents were eventually worn down by her persistent artistic efforts, the parental resistance may have had unknown effects in closing off certain professional opportunities for the budding artist. Certainly, the artist herself comments on the gendered nature of missed career opportunities, noting that "for a male DJ to have to become a parent there is an impact on his life, but there's not necessarily an impact on his career. That's the difference."

Having somewhat won the battle with her parents over the terrain of acceptable "lady-like" behaviour as a young woman, Mel Boogie went on to contend with gendered social expectations of the "good' mother. Who was she to insist on hosting a late night radio show and playing party music in club venues while having a child, and later two more at home? "It's still taking work," she says, "now that I'm a parent, I still have to work hard to show why I want to do it." Though Mel Boogie suggests her parents believed she should have given up her music activities after having her first child, she simply continued, largely aided by a supportive husband. Her tenacity has paid off. She has not taken significant breaks from the industry and has diversified her work to an array of spaces and formats—radio; DJing clubs and parties; maintaining an online blog and working on a website; she has integrated into Freedom Writers, a previously all male Hip-Hop crew; and has availed herself of a manager. She expresses her love of her music work as the one aspect of her day-to-day existence that she is able to maintain as hers alone in the context of motherhood, family and other wage labour. Mel Boogie's response suggests that her art and DJ work comprise a rare area of her life in which she is able to maintain an important relationship to the self, characterized by continuing artistic exploration. Hip-Hop is clearly the creative force in her life, an integral part of her that remains constant in the transitions that shape her personal experiences.

Mel Boogie's interview does not directly address sexism in the Hip-Hop music industry, and the artist is hesitant to articulate her experiences within a context of sexist victimization, whether in the realm of womanhood or motherhood. She begins by telling her interviewer that negotiating motherhood and her work in the music industry was not much of a consideration for her. That she would continue with her music was a taken for granted fact after the birth of her children. We also hear that early on, her experiences in the industry were marked by positive rather than negative differentiation (the novelty of being a woman DJ). However, Mel Boogie goes on to complicate this matter of fact rendering of her current success. She describes a supportive partnership with her husband (a Hip-Hop head himself), in which she is encouraged to seriously pursue her creative interests. She has also had the longstanding support of her older brother, a foundational figure in Canadian Hip-Hop culture. Unlike Lady P, Mel Boogie has had available to her a much stronger base of supportive, protective and experienced men in the industry—a reflection on the gendered nature of factors, that along with talent, frame women's careers as Hip-Hop artists. In the end, the support of her parents and spouse is of considerable significance in Mel Boogie's ability to juggle motherhood, marriage, full-time employment and a music career. And notwithstanding this support, she still notes the missed opportunities that necessarily accompany the negotiation of mothering and her artistic life, as well as the gendered aspects of these missed opportunities. The careers of men and women, according to Mel Boogie, are not equally impacted by the experience of parenthood. The careers of mothers take more hits than those of fathers, a reality that Mel Boogie accepts matter-of-factly. She attributes the inability to tour, an impediment to the full development of her music career, to the responsibilities of motherhood.

What is made clear in Mel Boogie's narrative is that her goal of contributing to the Hip-Hop community by building something of value in addition to her appearances as a DJ, call on the support and investment of the larger community itself in such a contribution. Families, friends, business associates, Hip-Hop fans and fellow artists of women like Mel Boogie will have to take notice of the important artistic and cultural contributions that flow out of the negotiations that such women artists make in growing Hip-Hop in the context of motherhood. Part of the difficulty in noticing this particular context of work in Hip-Hop culture has been the absence of a language with which to capture the complexity of mothering as a generative experience in Hip-Hop communities. Conventional representations of motherhood in commercial Hip-Hop would have us think of mothers along two problematically constructed and polarized frames. On the one, disparaged side, are all the "baby-mammas'; on the other, we find the elderly, asexual birth mothers on a pedestal. Between the two is the wife-to-be (wifey), ever teetering, on the verge of falling into the former category, and desperately clamouring, in the context of social expectations beyond her control, to eventually belong in the latter classification. Somewhere beneath and beyond these fabricated characters are women, many of them mothers, who channel a productive creative force that continues to shape and transform the context of Hip-Hop in communities across North America.

[1]CKLN is now an Internet radio station having had their license revoked in 2011 due to a number of CRTC violations.
[2]Kilowatt is the name of a mobile sound system from Mississauga, just outside the Toronto city limits.
[3]DJ Mel Boogie's older brother is Canada's first platinum Hip-Hop artist, Maestro Fresh Wes.
[4]CKLN is the public community radio for Ryerson University in downtown Toronto. In the era Lady P speaks of CKLN.
[5]Rap City was a weekly video show on MuchMusic, Canada's version of MTV.
[6]"Let Your Backbone Slide" was Maestro Fresh Wes' debut single in 1989.
[7]*E-Talk Daily* is a television show that focuses on current events in the entertainment business.
[8]On CHRY Mel Boogie was on the overnight slot called *Break-A-Dawn* when she first began her DJ career.
[9]Sylvia Robinson was responsible for the birth of renowned Old School Hip-Hop group the Sugarhill Gang (Chang).
[10]Sunshine Sound System was the dominant sound system in the Toronto area in the 1980s.
[11]Fly K and Mischievous C were two other female Emcees on the scene in the early 1980s.
[12]Caribana is Toronto's version of Trinidad's Carnival and is the largest

Carnival in North America, which originally started back in 1967 to celebrate Canada's 100th birthday.

[13]Marcia is DJ M&M from Kilowatt Sound Crew.

[14]Ron Nelson was the DJ and host of *The Fantastic Voyage*, one of Canada's earliest known Hip-Hop radio shows.

[15]Wes is short form for Maestro Fresh Wes, Canada's first platinum selling Hip-Hop artist.

[16]FLOW 93.5 is a commercial radio station in Toronto that was supposedly formatted to serve the city's Black populations from 2000 to 2010 when it was sold to a mainstream media conglomerate.

[17]The Stylus DJ awards are a national event in Canada that honours the country's best DJs from Hip-Hop, R&B and reggae music.

[18]Sunshine soundcrew was the undisputed, most popular soundcrew in Toronto in the 1980s.

[19]Honey Jam is an annual showcase of female talent in the music industry. It has been credited with helping to launch the careers of Nelly Furtado and Jully Black.

[20]Agile is the DJ for the Hip-Hop group Brassmunk.

[21]Canadian Music Week is an annual promotional event that celebrates Canadian music and features an industry-organized conference.

[22]DJ Mel Boogie organized a panel at the T-Dot Pioneers Exhibition in March 2010 entitled, "Where the Ladies @?"

[23]Black Entertainment Television is a popular primarily music video channel, now owned by Viacom.

[24]MuchMusic is a Canadian music video network.

[25]Many consider Starting From Scratch the top mix DJ in Toronto. He DJs for FLOW 93.5 FM.

WORKS CITED

Chang, Jeff. *Can't Stop, Won't Stop: A History of the Hip-Hop Generation*. New York: Macmillan, 2005.

Rose, Tricia. *Black Noise: Rap Music and Black Culture in Contemporary America*. Honover: Wesleyan University Press, 1994.

Contributor Notes

Shana L. Calixte is the Executive Director of NISA/Northern Initiative for Social Action in Sudbury, a grassroots mental health organization. She also teaches part-time in the Department of Women's Studies at Laurentian University. She is completing her Ph.D. at York University, with academic work focusing on the history of Caribbean Girl Guide associations and HIV/AIDS education. Shana lives with her partner and their two sons in Sudbury.

Mark V. Campbell is a Post-Doctoral Fellow at the University of Guelph in the Improvisation, Community and Social Practice Research Project. His current research interests include turntablism, Canadian Hip-Hop culture, Afrodiasporic cultures, Black Canada, Afrosonic theory and community arts development.

Travis L. Gosa is Assistant Professor of Social Science at Cornell University. He holds faculty appointments in the graduate fields of Africana Studies and Education, and is affiliated with the Cornell Center for the Study of Inequality. He received his Ph.D. in Sociology from The Johns Hopkins University in 2008, along with a Certificate in Social Inequality. He has been an education policy analyst at both the Maryland State Department of Education and American Institutes for Research in Washington, D.C. Prof. Gosa teaches courses on race, education, Hip-Hop, and the African American family. Gosa's recent essays have been published in *Teacher's College Record*, *Journal of Popular Music Studies*, *Popular Music and Society*, and *The Journal of American Culture*.

Alexis Pauline Gumbs earned her Ph.D. in English, African and African American Studies and Women and Gender Studies at Duke University. Her dissertation entitled '*We Can Learn to Mother Ourselves': The Queer Survival of Black Feminism,* elaborates on the concepts of queer mothering discussed in this chapter. She is also the author of *Emergency Broadcast,* a youth activism Hip-Hop workbook, and many articles and reviews about Hip-Hop and popular culture. Alexis is now engaged in a national multimedia community education documentary film project called the MobileHomecoming Project, which is dedicated to amplifying generations of queer Black brilliance and building intergenerational relationships in the Black queer community. She is also the instigator of the Eternal Summer of the Black Feminist Mind multimedia educational movement, based in Durham, North Carolina. Alexis has been honored as one of *UTNE Reader's* 50 Visionaries Transforming the World, a Reproductive Health Heroine by Reproductive Health Reality Check and nominated as a Black Woman Rising by Black Women's Blueprint, and featured in *Curve Magazine.*

Ruth Henry (MC OASIS) is a Hip-Hop artist, educator, and activist, as well as the proud mother of two amazing daughters. Originally hailing from Boston, Mass., she currently resides in Cartagena, Colombia, where she is a member of the all-female Hip-Hop collective Matriarkao and coordinates La Lengua de mi Barrio, a Hip-Hop exchange program between the United States and Colombia with an emphasis on nonviolent resistance as a path towards social justice. After graduating from Hampshire College in 1999, she continued her non-academic education by traveling to many different countries, engaging in community and youth organizing in Boston, and participating in a variety of artistic and justice-based trainings. In 2002 she traveled to Colombia for the first time on a Fulbright grant, where she self-produced her first album, Puntos de Luz. Since then she has launched the demo "Movimiento" and participated in Matriarkao's first mixtape. She has been featured on the albums of both national and international artists such as El Viejo Nandes, Lady Enchantress, Mary Hellen, and Gambitto, and has performed in a wide array of venues ranging from Miami to Medellin to Palestine. She has also worked to use the arts to bring youth together across conflicts in programs such as the Cacique Youth Arts Program and Project Hip-Hop in Boston and has taught arts and language at Sanbuenaventura University and the University of Cartagena in Colombia. She is currently working on a full-length solo album entitled: *Overstand Aggression Standing Inwardly Strong*. You can find her first video on YouTube: "MC Oasis- Homenaje/Ode."

Maki Motapanyane is Assistant Professor of Women's Studies at Mount Royal University. She has published in the areas of feminist theory, transnational feminist research, and cultural studies. Her research is focused on feminism in Africa, and gender and international development. She is the busy mother of two school-aged children.

Sharon Miller (Pri the Honey Dark) and **Shantelena Mouzon (Helixx C. Armageddon)** are core members of the New York based all-women Hip-Hop collective Anomolies. Pri is an Emcee and producer. She is active in Hip-Hop culture in the U.S., having earned numerous local and national awards for her talent. Helixx is an Emcee and lyricist who has also gained widespread national recognition for her artistic skill. Along with fellow core members Kuttin Kandi, Big Tara and Invincible, the Anomolies crew has created an important social and professional network for independent female Hip-Hop artists in North America.

Erik Nielson is a Ph.D. candidate in English at the University of Sheffield. His current research covers a wide range of African American literary and musical traditions, with a particular emphasis on rap. His work has appeared or is forthcoming in *African American Review, Journal of Black Studies, Journal of Popular Music Studies, International Journal of Cultural Studies, Western Journal of Black Studies,* and *Popular Communication.*

Nicholas Powers is Assistant Professor of English at SUNY Old Westbury. He is also a freelance reporter who has written for the *Village Voice,* The Indypendent and Vibe.com. His poetry book *Theater of War* was published by Upset Press in 2004.